STUDYING WITH
MISS BISHOP

Studying with Miss Bishop

MEMOIRS FROM A
YOUNG WRITER'S LIFE

DANA GIOIA

PAUL DRY BOOKS
Philadelphia 2021

First Paul Dry Books Edition, 2021

Paul Dry Books, Inc.
Philadelphia, Pennsylvania
www.pauldrybooks.com

Printed in the United States of America

Library of Congress Control Number: 2020946648

ALSO BY DANA GIOIA

POETRY

Daily Horoscope
The Gods of Winter
Interrogations at Noon
Pity the Beautiful
99 Poems: New and Selected

CRITICAL COLLECTIONS

Can Poetry Matter?: Essays on Poetry and American Culture
*The Barrier of a Common Language: Essays on Contemporary
    British Poetry*
Disappearing Ink: Poetry at the End of Print Culture
The Catholic Writer Today: and Other Essays

TRANSLATIONS

Mottetti: Poems of Love by Eugenio Montale
The Madness of Hercules by Seneca

OPERA LIBRETTI

Nosferatu
Tony Caruso's Final Broadcast
The Three Feathers
Haunted

For my brother Ted
&
his namesake
Theodore Ortiz

ACKNOWLEDGMENTS

Versions of these pieces first appeared in the *New Yorker*, the *Hudson Review*, *American Scholar*, *Cumberland Poetry Review*, *Boulevard*, and *Witness*. They have been extensively revised and expanded for this volume. The author wishes to thank the editors who accommodated his missed deadlines, compulsive revisions, and general disregard for assigned word count. He also wishes to thank John Paul Russo for verifying details of Ronald Perry's life. God bless them every one.

CONTENTS

PREFACE

Studying with Miss Bishop is a book of literary memoirs, portraits of six people whose examples helped me become a writer. Four were famous authors—Elizabeth Bishop, John Cheever, Robert Fitzgerald, and James Dickey. The other two were unknown—my Mexican uncle, who served as a Merchant Marine until his early death, and Ronald Perry, a forgotten poet whom I never met. If that cast of characters seems strange, it's because literary life is strange.

The first piece describes my odd and bookish childhood in a Los Angeles apartment surrounded by the library of my dead uncle. This unlikely legacy set in motion the equally unlikely course of my adult life. The later chapters provide portraits of each author. I have tried to give the reader a tangible sense of what it was like to be in their company. They were people of potent personality. I paid attention to them. In some cases, I even kept notes. I felt others would enjoy meeting them as I did.

Preparing this book for publication, I was struck by how much the literary world has changed since the events I describe, most of which occurred in the

1970s. In those exhilarating years, still electrified by the energy of the late sixties, my generation felt we lived on the edge of the future. Now that period has become an historical era. In telling a story, John Cheever once remarked that it took place in a time when men still wore hats. In that spirit, let me say that my reminiscences take place when people still wrote letters and read newspapers. There were still phone booths, newsstands, and typewriters. Every neighborhood had a bookstore. No one owned a computer, and telephones were attached to walls by wires. Education meant books. Cultural opinion was shaped by magazines and quarterlies. Many writers were genuine celebrities. Men did not wear hats, but many still smoked, and most wore leather shoes. That world will require explaining to the future. Without trying to write period pieces, I endeavored to convey the atmosphere of the era. I enjoyed remembering a time when the printed word still had such power.

This book grew slowly. I wrote early versions of the memoirs many years ago when the events were still fresh in my memory. I kept revising and expanding the material to capture each personality and setting. Although I'm now on the brink of old age, the events I describe happened early in my life—mostly in my twenties before I had published a book. I was either a student or an office worker.

At twenty I suffered from a common juvenile disease: I wanted to be a poet. I recognized even then my complaint would prove incurable. What to do about it? The temptation was to stay in school forever—first to study, then to teach. Academia seemed the only practical course. Nothing in my background provided any perspective on an artistic career. I was the first person in my family to go to college. I had never met anyone who made a living as a writer. Even as an undergraduate at Stanford, the only poets I knew were fellow students. I went to graduate school to be a poet. All poets taught, right? I loved graduate work—the scholarship, the argumentation, the theory. What could be more fun than reading and talking about books?

The trouble was that Harvard was training me to be a research university professor of literature. It was a fascinating place. I learned to talk, think, and write in a certain way—informed, analytical, meticulous. Such rigor ran the risk of pedantry, but that was assumed to be the necessary cost of accuracy. This mandarin idiom took pride in excluding the uninitiated. The more I mastered these analytical disciplines, however, the more detached I became from the intuitive faculties out of which I wrote poetry. My underdeveloped native instincts stood no chance against the collective mental prowess of Harvard.

The professions we enter change the ways in which we look at the world and ourselves. I recognized my sense of being a poet was changing in ways alien to my sense of the art, which was neither cerebral nor elitist. I didn't want to write in ways that excluded people, especially the people I came from. They lacked education, but most were quick and clever. I admired poets, such as Shakespeare, Hardy, and Frost, who could address a mixed audience without condescension. I appreciated the skill and study good poetry required, but I felt the final poem shouldn't stink of midnight oil. I wanted my poems to be moving, memorable, and accessible—not to everyone but certainly to all intelligent and alert readers whatever their background. I imagined a style that would speak both to my fellow poets and the common reader. However inchoate, that was my early ambition. Unfortunately, I had no real notion how to become such a writer.

There was a conventional answer to my dilemma—get a graduate degree in Creative Writing—but I never considered that alternative. The best way to escape a graduate school in literature wasn't to enter another program in literature. To my own surprise, I no longer wanted to be a professor; I wanted to be a poet. But what did that mean? I was already writing poems. The question was how to make them better—truer, deeper, intoxicating. I had always been different from my schoolmates. I imagined that the poems I needed to write would be different, too. I didn't think I'd find the right ways to express my idiosyncrasies in a writing workshop.

There is a famous anecdote about the great linguist Roman Jakobson. When Harvard considered hiring Vladimir Nabokov to teach Russian literature, Jakobson nixed the idea because Nabokov lacked an advanced degree. "Gentlemen," he told the hiring committee, "Even if we allow he is an important writer, are we next to invite an elephant to be Professor of Zoology?" At Harvard, I had the good luck to study with two magnificent elephants—Bishop and Fitzgerald. They were indeed different creatures from my other professors. Both had led literary careers outside the university. Both had come to teaching late in life. A year later I met John Cheever who had not even gone to college. This remarkable trio proved that one didn't need to teach to be a writer. I knew that Wallace Stevens and T. S. Eliot had made their way while working in business. If they could do it, maybe I could, too. And so I left the academic world of literature to figure things out on my own.

How does someone learn to write? Certainly, one has to master language and explore the medium by wide reading. One must practice and develop the craft of writing. But there is also the challenge of style. Finding one's style means something beyond learning conventional ways of putting words together for certain effects—minimalist, hard-boiled, stream-of-consciousness, surreal. Style means knowing who you are and how you feel about your own experience. Robert Frost remarked that "style in prose or verse is that which indicates how the writer takes himself and what he is saying . . . the way he carries himself toward his ideas and deeds." That skill is not easily learned in a writing workshop.

Style isn't just a literary accomplishment; it's a human one. Some people achieve a strong and certain sense of themselves early. I did not. I had moved so far beyond my origins I hardly knew where I was. I was a poet raised mostly by people who didn't speak English as their first language. The intellectual skills were never a problem. I knew books and literature. That was the easy part. What I didn't know was how to lead a writer's life. I couldn't learn that from books. I needed living examples, especially people I liked and admired.

Goethe once remarked that to be lucky at the beginning was everything. I was lucky in my family, and then, as I first recognized my literary vocation, I was lucky again in the writers I met. I've composed these memoirs to convey my gratitude. *Studying with Miss Bishop* is a book about learning to write through friendship. I doubt these people understood how much they gave me. They were just being themselves, but that was just what I needed to get started.

Lonely Impulse of Delight

ONE READER'S CHILDHOOD

Courtesy Dana Gioia

Every reader has two lives—one public, the other secret. The public life is the one visible to teachers, friends, and families, though none of them ever sees it fully. It consists of homes and houses, schools and schoolmates, friends and enemies, lovers, colleagues, and competitors. This is the realm of experience universally known as real life. But every true reader has a secret life, which is equally intense, complex, and important. The books we read are no different from the people we meet or the cities we visit. Some books, people, or places hardly matter, others change our lives. No one else will ever read, reread, or misread the same books in the same way or in the same order. Our inner lives are as rich and real as our outer lives, even if they remain mostly unknowable to others. Perhaps that is why books matter so much. They serve as intimate companions. Some books guide us. Others lead us astray. A few rescue or redeem us. All of them confide something of the wonder, joy, terror, and mystery of being alive.

I had a happy, lonely childhood characterized by many odd circumstances—two of which turned me into a passionate lifelong reader. First, both of my parents had full-time jobs, sometimes even two jobs. Among working-class Latin families fifty years ago, this situation was not only unusual but also slightly embarrassing, suggesting a certain financial desperation—not altogether mistaken in our case. Consequently, I spent a great deal of time alone in our apartment or sat awake with one of my parents asleep while the other was at work. (They worked entirely different hours.) The second odd circumstance was our apartment, which was full of books—not popular paperbacks or book-club selections, but serious hardbound volumes of fiction, poetry, drama, philosophy, art, and music. These books did not reflect my parents' interests. They read very little except newspapers and magazines. The large, eclectic, and intellectually distinguished library was the legacy of my mother's brother, Ted Ortiz, who had died in an airplane crash when I was six. An old-style proletarian intellectual, my uncle had served in the Merchant Marine and lived with my parents when he was not at sea.

Special shelves housed the heavier volumes—including more than a hundred bound folio scores, printed in Germany, of the complete works of Mozart, Beethoven, Brahms, Bach, and Haydn. (Tall plywood cabinets likewise lined one wall of our tiny garage holding hundreds of classical record albums.) Many books were in foreign languages—Dante in Italian, Goethe in German, Cervantes in Spanish. These were family books, not the possessions of a stranger or a school. They belonged to us, even if we didn't know what to do with them.

I grew up in a tight enclave of Sicilian relations. My family lived in the large back apartment of a stucco triplex. Next door was a nearly identical triplex. Five of these six apartments were inhabited by relations, including my grandparents, my aunt and uncle, and various cousins. Other relations lived nearby. The older people had been born in Sicily and had made their arduous and often painful way to Los Angeles via New York City and Detroit. An Italian dialect was spoken when the older generation was in the room. Conversation shifted to English when they left. Although born in Detroit, my father had spoken no English until he started school. Most of my schoolmates in Hawthorne, California, came from similar backgrounds, though their families spoke Spanish. In my parish all grandparents spoke English with a foreign accent—if they spoke English at all.

None of my practical, hard-working relations read much, but neither did they disdain the activity. There were a few books in their homes, but they were mostly inexpensive encyclopedias and young adult classics—books bought, that is, for someone else to read. I never saw anyone open one of these decorative volumes except myself jealously examining them on a visit. In fact, during my entire childhood I don't recall ever seeing any adult relation, except my mother, read a book. Everyone was busy cooking, cleaning, building, or repairing something. Leisure time was spent together—eating, talking, or playing cards—not going off alone with a book. Kitchen table arguments were especially popular. Everyone argued about politics, religion, money, sports, and people. No one minded these often fiery debates. The only thing that disturbed people was being ignored.

My family had no idea what to make of my bookish habits, but they never mocked or discouraged them. Never before having encountered a bookworm, these stoical Sicilians hoped for the best. One reason Latin families stay tight is that they allow their members latitude for personal taste. Italians also admire any highly developed special skill—carpentry, cooking, gardening, singing, even reading. The best skills helped one make a living. The others helped one enjoy living.

My parents rarely brought home children's books, so my earliest memories of reading include taking down the uniformly black-bound novels of Thomas Mann or the green-bound plays of George Bernard Shaw looking vainly for something a kid might enjoy. Childhood was slower before cable television, videogames, iPhones, and the Internet. Kids had time on their hands. We had to entertain ourselves, which meant exploring every possible means of amusement our circumscribed lives afforded. I paged through every book on every shelf, however unlikely its appeal. I loved my uncle's *Victor Book of Opera* with its photographs and engravings of old singers and set designs. I constructed my own plots for the operas based on these illustrations. I also grew up seeing reproductions of Botticelli, Michelangelo, Titian, Velazquez, and El Greco, mostly in black and white, before I ever saw the drawings of Dr. Seuss or his peers.

There were few religious books in our deeply Roman Catholic home. My parents owned only the Bible, *The Lives of the Saints*, several pocket-sized missals, and a single, inspirational paperback by Bishop Fulton Sheen. Although my Mexican uncle, a former Communist, had converted to Catholicism shortly before his sudden death, he had left no devotional texts, only books on comparative religion. I suspect that no other Sicilian or Mexican home in Hawthorne possessed a copy of the Koran. The family Bible proved a keen disappointment. This situation was no fault of God's word, only its inept illustrator. Our bulky, cheap edition contained two dozen color prints that were so awful that even a ten-year-old felt cheated. I found spiritual sustenance only in *The Lives of the Saints*, especially in its vivid accounts of legendary hermits and martyrs. This early imaginative nourishment explains far more about my inner life than I care to disclose.

Although I perused the title pages of *Heartbreak House* and *The Magic Mountain*, I never read them until college. I loved the books that boys love—stories of wonder, danger, and adventure. Among the earliest books I remember reading were young adult biographies of Julius Caesar, Alexander the Great, Joan of Arc, Marco Polo, Napoleon, and John Paul Jones, which were sold at the local toy store. (I had been alerted to Caesar's existence by a Classics Illustrated comic book.) Exhausting those volumes, I moved into the adult history section of the local library. It may seem odd that in fourth grade my favorite book was Caesar's *Gallic Wars*, but I was an odd child, and I can still remember the number of soldiers who fought on each side of the Roman general's major battles.

I delighted in books on mythology, especially Norse mythology, and devoured prose versions of *Beowulf*, the *Iliad*, the *Odyssey*, and *The Song of Roland*. (I had no idea then that these stories had originally been written in verse.) I also read and reread the elegant retellings of myths by Edith Hamilton, Thomas Bulfinch, and Padraic Colum. Few children's authors today write prose as well as Hamilton or Colum did. In fourth grade I discovered unabridged editions of *Gulliver's Travels* and *Robinson Crusoe* in St. Joseph's tiny parochial school library, which was about the size of a large walk-in closet. No one told me the novels were too hard for a ten-year-old. I devoured them, and then passed them on to my best friend.

Toward the end of fourth grade I had one of my decisive experiences as a reader—my first great literary love affair. I came across a copy of Edgar Rice Burroughs's *At the Earth's Core* on the paperback rack of the corner drugstore. I liked the exciting cover so I plunked down forty cents and took the book home. It was, I joyfully discovered, the perfect novel—brilliantly plotted and full of action. Over the next few years I read everything I could find by Burroughs— except the perfunctory later Tarzan novels. I also got two of my parochial school friends hooked, Paul Lucero and Ernie Rael.

We practiced literary criticism in its purest form—talking about and comparing the books we read in common. We held a general consensus that Burroughs's first three Mars novels were his master-pieces, with the first two Tarzan novels only slightly less thrilling. I still find it exciting to remember the titles and luridly exuberant covers of those Ace and Ballantine paperbacks—*Pellucidar, The Land that Time Forgot, Pirates of Venus, A Princess of Mars,* and *The Mad King.* I read at least forty of Burroughs's novels, and I have had the pleasure of rereading the Mars, Venus, and early Tarzan novels aloud to my sons—now mar-veling less at the author's breathless plotting than at the huge vocabulary popular writers once took for granted among young readers.

I developed a passion for science fiction, adven-ture, and fantasy literature. A few of my favorite boy-hood writers have now, I am sorry to say, entered the fringe of the academic canon. In my heart, however, they remain forever beyond the reach of pedagogic good taste—H. P. Lovecraft, H. G. Wells, Ray Brad-bury, Olaf Stapledon, Arthur C. Clarke, and Isaac Asimov—as well as the now mostly forgotten Rich-ard Matheson, Charles Beaumont, Charles G. Finney, and William Hope Hodgson. It was, in fact, dystopian sci-fi that got me interested in literary fiction. I read Aldous Huxley, Kurt Vonnegut, and George Orwell initially as sci-fi writers, and only then discovered their literary novels. To a working-class teenage Angeleno, who knew nothing first-hand of the larger world, I must confess that Huxley's futuristic fantasies, *Brave New World* and *Ape and Essence*, were novels I easily understood, but his realistic social comedies, *Crome Yellow* and *Antic Hay*, were obscure and mysterious. Mars I comprehended, but an English country house was an alien world.

In fifth grade, I became interested in art after seeing television specials on Leonardo da Vinci and Michelangelo. I haunted the enormous Hawthorne public library and over the next four years voraciously read through hundreds of art books. I studied European painting the way other boys immersed themselves in sports statistics. I daydreamed about visiting the Alte Pinakothek, Hermitage, Uffizi, and Prado. At twelve, I could tell you the location of every Vermeer, Giotto, or Bosch in the world and—weirder still—could identify the provenance of most paintings in Washington's National Gallery, which I had never visited. I read S. N. Behrman's biography of the art dealer Joseph Duveen three times and kept track of Old Master auction prices in a little notebook. I spent the money I earned doing odd jobs by ordering museum catalogues and subscribing to *Art News* and *Connoisseur*. (One continuing pleasure of adulthood has been to visit the museums whose catalogues I studied as a child.) My parents approved of my odd behavior because they associated my interest in art with academic achievement—just as they associated my science fiction and fantasy reading with laziness and impracticality.

I must stress two crucial facts. First, no one—neither a relative nor a teacher—ever encouraged my reading or intellectual pursuits. Second, my bookish hobbies (except for science fiction) needed to be hidden from my friends. I never confided my passion for art to anyone at school. Luckily, none of my classmates ever seemed to visit the library, so my double life remained safe from their discovery. I was grateful for my anonymity. While I didn't need encouragement, I also felt no urge to court disapproval. Discretion was the better part of valor. My childhood secrecy proved good training. This pattern of a double life—one public, the other one imaginative—was repeated in adulthood when I worked in the business world while secretly writing poetry at night.

I have always been an insomniac. Even as a young boy, I had trouble falling asleep. My parents, both night owls, let their children keep late hours. Once we were in bed, they never forced us to turn off the lights—one of their countless kindnesses. Consequently, every night I read in bed, often for hours. When I remember my childhood reading, I see myself in Sears and Roebuck pajamas, propped up under the covers, devouring *The Circus of Dr. Lao*, *The Time Machine*, or *The Lost World* while my younger brother Ted sleeps in the twin bed beside me. I usually kept the next book I planned to read on my nightstand—not so much as an incentive to finish my current selection but simply to provide anticipatory pleasure. "My library was dukedom large enough," Prospero says in

The Tempest, and so seemed the kingdom of my childhood. The clock would tick toward midnight and beyond while I wandered through Rome and London, Lilliput and Mars. Today I am a world traveler, but life never seemed larger than in that tiny lamplit room.

In my childhood milieu, reading was associated with self-improvement. I suppose this uplifting motive played some role in my intellectual pursuits, but my insatiable appetite for books came mostly from curiosity and pleasure. I liked to read. I liked to investigate and study subjects that interested me—European painting, silent films, dinosaurs, great battles, and mythology. My interests changed and developed year by year. Some of the books I read were quite respectable, such as *Gulliver's Travels* or Vasari's *Lives of the Artists*, but respectability never guided my choices.

By the standards of Hawthorne, a rough and ugly industrial town, my love of books was clearly excessive, indeed almost shameful. Not able to control the passion, I needed to hide it, if only to keep it pure. A private passion is free from public pressures. Then I could follow this "lonely impulse of delight," to borrow a phrase from William Butler Yeats, wherever it led. I read good books for enjoyment just as I did each issue of *Spiderman*, *The Incredible Hulk*, or the *Fantastic Four*. I can't think of better ways to learn than through pleasure and curiosity. I guess the reason these two qualities play so small a role in formal education is that they are so subjective and individual. Curiosity and delight can't be institutionalized.

Childhood and adolescence form our sensibilities. By the time I arrived in college, I had already developed a deep suspicion of all theories of art that did not originate in pleasure. Surely, this conviction developed from my own self-education in books, and in particular from exploring them with little tutorial assistance—except from an uncle who could not speak to me, except though the mute juxtaposition of subjects in his book collection.

My uncle must have been a remarkable man. Although raised in brutal poverty, he had supported himself at sea from the age of fifteen while also learning five languages and schooling himself in music, literature, and art. I don't honestly remember him—only stories about him and a few photographs. If I claimed to love him, I would really be saying that I loved the books and records he left behind. I'm not sure the distinction matters. I think I know him pretty well. After all, he helped raise me.

Studying with
Miss Bishop

Photograph by Rollie McKenna © Rosalie Thorpe McKenna Foundation

In February 1975 I began my last semester as a graduate student in English at Harvard University. Picking my courses that final term, I tried for once to pick them carefully, and I came down to a choice between two teachers—Robert Lowell and Elizabeth Bishop. Mr. Lowell's seminar on nineteenth-century poets was very popular. Everyone who fancied himself a poet talked about taking it. As for Elizabeth Bishop's course on modern poetry, I had never heard anyone mention it at all. It seemed to exist only in the course catalogue: "English 285: Studies in Modern Poetry: Miss Elizabeth Bishop, Instructor."

In retrospect, one might imagine that it would have been nearly impossible to get into one of Elizabeth Bishop's classes. But this was not the case. Her course was not one of the many that Harvard students fought to get into and afterward always managed to mention they had taken. The most popular teachers among the young literary elite were Robert Lowell, William Alfred, Robert Fitzgerald, and the newly arrived Alexander Theroux. On the first day of their classes, it was difficult just to squeeze into the room. While Northrop Frye, who was visiting Harvard that year to deliver the Norton Lectures, drew audiences of nearly a thousand for his class on myth and literature, Miss Bishop, I was to learn, rarely attracted more than a dozen unenthusiastic undergraduates.

Her manner was at odds with the academic glamour of Harvard, her conversation not designed to impress. She was a politely formal, shy, and undramatic woman. She wanted no worshipful circle of students, and got none. Only her writing course was popular, but all writing courses were in great demand at Harvard, since the university as a matter of policy offered very few. While the Cambridge literary establishment held Miss Bishop in the highest esteem, among the undergraduates she was just another writer on the faculty. They knew she was well known, but wasn't everyone who taught at Harvard?

Miss Bishop's first session was held in a classroom on the second floor of Sever Hall, a grimy building of supposed architectural distinction in the Harvard Yard. The classroom—narrow, poorly whitewashed, with high, cracked ceilings—looked as if it belonged in an abandoned high school in North Dakota. There were exposed radiator pipes with peeling paint. A few battered shelves were lined with broken-spined textbooks of incalculable age. A couple of dozen chairs, few of them matching, were set randomly around a huge, scratched table, at one end of which—prim, impeccably coiffured, and smoking—sat Miss Elizabeth Bishop.

I recognized her immediately from photographs I had seen in books, but somehow, suddenly coming into a room where she was sitting a few feet away, I was taken by surprise. At that point in my life, I had seen so few real poets in person that I felt a strange shock at being in the same room as someone whose work I knew on the page. It was an odd, almost uncomfortable sensation to have the perfect world of books peer so casually into the disorder of everyday life. I was also surprised by her appearance. She seemed disappointingly normal. I don't know exactly what I had expected—perhaps someone slightly bohemian or noticeably eccentric, a Marianne Moore or a Margaret Rutherford. Instead, I saw a very attractive woman in what I guessed to be her middle fifties (actually, she was sixty-four), dressed in a tasteful, expensive-looking suit, perfectly poised, waiting to begin. By the time the class started, only about a dozen students had arrived. I was surprised at so small a turnout. Moreover, we sat scattered around the room in a way that made the class seem half empty rather than intimate.

Eventually, she began. "I am Elizabeth Bishop," she announced, "and this is Studies in Modern Poetry. The way I usually run this class is by asking the students to choose three or four poets they would like to read and talk about. Does anyone have a suggestion?"

The first question was always an important moment in a Harvard class. It set the tone of the session, like the opening bid on the New York Stock Exchange.

"Can we read John Ashbery? Something like 'Self-Portrait in a Convex Mirror'?" a young man asked from the back of the room.

Now, this was a truly exceptional question. Ashbery was just becoming well known, and every young poet I knew had been reading him. But hardly anyone was able to understand Ashbery. His work was so elusive and difficult that people who talked authoritatively about it were held in universally high regard.

"Ashbery?" said Miss Bishop. "Oh, no, we can't read Ashbery. I wouldn't know what to say about him."

"Couldn't we try an early book?" the student said.

"No, no. Let's try someone else."

"What about Auden?" another student asked.

"Oh, I love Auden, but we can't do him."

"Why not?"

"We just read him in my other class. We should read new people."

She acted as if we knew exactly what authors she had assigned the previous semester. I felt at ease. At least she was disorganized. I didn't have to revise my stereotype of poets entirely.

That first session must have seemed particularly unpromising. By the second class, the dozen original students had dwindled down to five—four undergraduates and me. The administration responded by moving us into a more intimate facility—the "seminar room" in the basement of Kirkland House. One entered by finding a well-hidden side door in one of the dormitory's wings, descending several staircases, and then wandering about until one came upon a vast, colorless room full of unwanted furniture and dismembered bicycles. There were pipes on the ceiling, and an endless Ping-Pong game went on behind a thin partition. In one corner stood a table slightly larger than a card table, and that was the only usable table in the place. Eventually we all found the room, and the six of us took our places facing one another across the tiny surface.

"I'm not a very good teacher," Miss Bishop began. "So to make sure you learn something in this class I am going to ask each of you to memorize at least ten lines a week from one of the poets we are reading." Had she announced that we were all required to attend class in sackcloth and ashes, the undergraduates could not have looked more horrified. This was the twentieth century, the age of criticism.

"Memorize poems?" someone asked. "But why?"

"So that you'll learn something in spite of me."

People exchanged knowing glances, as if to say, "We're dealing with a real oddball." But the subject was closed.

Her modesty was entirely sincere. She was the most self-effacing writer I have ever met. She had her own opinions and preferences, but there was no false pride in her. Several times in almost every class, she would throw up her hands and say, "I have no idea what this line means. Can anybody figure it out?" And all of us would then scuffle ineffectually to her rescue.

Teaching did not come naturally to her. She was almost sixty when she became an instructor at Harvard, and one could sense how uneasy she felt in the role. She would not lecture to us even informally. Sessions with her were not so much classes as conversations. She would ask someone to read a poem aloud. If it was a long poem, then each of us would read a stanza in turn. (At times, it reminded me of a reading class in grammar school.) Then we would talk about the poem line by line in a relaxed, unorganized way. She rarely made an attempt to summarize any observations at the end of discussions. She enjoyed pointing out the particulars of each poem, not generalizing about it, and she insisted that we understand every individual word, even if we had no idea what the poem was about as a whole. "Use the dictionary," she said once. "It's better than the critics."

She had no system in approaching poems, and her practice of close reading had little in common with the disciplines of New Criticism. She did not attempt to tie the details of a poem together into a tight structure. She would have found that notion unappealing. Nor did she see poems in any strict historical perspective. Good poems existed for her in a sort of eternal present. Studying poetry with her was a leisurely process. The order of the words in the poem was the only agenda, and we would go from word to word, from line to line, as if we had all the time in the world. We only read poems she liked, and it was a pleasure at Harvard to have a teacher who, however baffled she might be in managing her class, clearly enjoyed the things she was talking about.

We began with poems from *Spring and All*, by William Carlos Williams. We worked through each poem as slowly as if it had been written in a foreign language, and Miss Bishop provided a detailed commentary: biographical information, publication dates, geographical facts, and personal anecdotes about her meetings with the poet. She particularly admired the passage with which Williams opened the title poem, "Spring and All":

> By the road to the contagious hospital
> under the surge of the blue
> mottled clouds driven from the
> northeast—a cold wind. Beyond, the
> waste of broad, muddy fields
> brown with dried weeds, standing and fallen
>
> patches of standing water
> the scattering of tall trees
>
> All along the road the reddish
> purplish, forked, upstanding, twiggy
> stuff of bushes and small trees
> with dead, brown leaves under them
> leafless vines—

It took us about an hour to work through this straightforward passage, not because Miss Bishop had any thesis to prove but because it reminded her of so many things—wildflowers, New Jersey, the medical profession, modern painting. Her remarks often went beyond the point at hand, but frequently she made some phrase or passage we might have overlooked in the poem come alive through a brilliant, unexpected observation. For example, later in the poem Williams has four lines about plants coming up in the early spring:

> They enter the new world naked,
> cold, uncertain of all
> save that they enter. All about them
> the cold, familiar wind—

"Williams is using a human metaphor for the plants," Miss Bishop explained. "As a doctor, he specialized in obstetrics, and here he sees the plants as if they were babies being born."

The poem of Williams's that she enjoyed talking about most was "The Sea-Elephant," which begins:

> Trundled from
> the strangeness of the sea—
> a kind of
> heaven—
>
> Ladies and Gentlemen!
> the greatest
> sea-monster ever exhibited
> alive
>
> the gigantic
> sea-elephant! O wallow

of flesh where
are

there fish enough for
that
appetite stupidity
cannot lessen?

One thing she found particularly fascinating about the poem was the way Williams made transitions. The poem moves quickly from one voice to the next, from one mood to another. It switches effortlessly from wonder to pathos, then to burlesque, and then back to wonder. I think this was the side of Williams's work closest to Bishop's own poetry. She, too, was a master of swift, unexpected transitions, and her poems move as surprisingly from amusement to wonder, from quiet pathos to joy. But with "The Sea-Elephant" the subject alone was enough to light up her interest. She loved talking about exotic animals or flowers, and, not surprisingly, she proved formidably well informed about sea elephants. And she admitted that for her the high point of the poem was the word that Williams invented to imitate the sea elephant's roar: "Blouaugh." It was music to her ears.

We began reading Wallace Stevens's work, and started with "The Man on the Dump." Here, too, I think the choice was revealing. She often named the poets who influenced her most as George Herbert, Gerard Manley Hopkins, Marianne Moore, and Stevens, and a poem like "The Man on the Dump" represents the side of Stevens's work most like her own. While the poem is pure Stevens in its central concerns, it is slightly uncharacteristic in style. The rhythms are freer and more unpredictable than the blank verse poems it superficially resembles. The tone is wry and quiet, the organization smooth and conversational, not pseudo-dramatic. The catalogues of rubbish and flowers it contains are more typical of Bishop than of Stevens:

> Days pass like papers from a press.
> The bouquets come here in the papers. So the sun,
> And so the moon, both come, and the janitor's poems
> Of every day, the wrapper on the can of pears,
> The cat in the paper-bag, the corset, the box
> From Esthonia: the tiger chest, for tea.

Miss Bishop was more interested in Stevens's music than his philosophy, and she became most animated in discussing poems that bordered on inspired nonsense verse, where meaning was secondary to sound. She not only felt uncomfortable analyzing Stevens's ideas, she didn't even enjoy his more abstract works. Paging through Stevens's *Collected Poems* one afternoon, trying to figure out the next week's reading list, she claimed she wouldn't assign us a long, speculative poem, "The Comedian as the Letter C," because she couldn't stand to read it another time.

The only poem she specifically ordered us to memorize was Stevens's "The Emperor of Ice-Cream," and the next week she sat patiently through five stumbling recitations before leading us into a long discussion. Characteristically, she wanted us to memorize the poem before we talked about its meaning. To her, the images and the music of the lines were primary. If we comprehended the sound, eventually we would understand the sense. I also suspect that she stressed memorization in her class because it was one of the ways she herself approached poems. She knew many of Stevens's poems by heart and would quote them casually in conversation. She recited them like universally known maxims any of us might have brought up had we only thought of them first. Her impromptu recitations charmed us. They had a playful intimacy not often present in her class. She was shocked on the occasions when we did not recognize the poem she quoted. It was not the only way we disappointed her.

To Miss Bishop, Stevens's greatest subject was not poetry, the supreme fiction. It was Florida, the supreme landscape. She introduced us to Stevens with a long discourse on Florida—"the state with the prettiest name," she said—and returned to the subject repeatedly, always with affection and enthusiasm. But in a strange way her memories of Florida had become as Platonic an ideal as Stevens's visions of order at Key West. She was painfully aware of how much of *her* Florida had vanished. Her comments on Key West were always prefaced with disclaimers like "Back in the thirties, there used to be . . ." She spoke of it as if she were Eve remembering Eden.

"More delicate than the historians' are the map-makers' colors," she once wrote, and, appropriately, she began her discussion of Key West with a topo-graphical act. "Key West," she told us, "is only ninety miles from Cuba." (Writing this down in my class-room notes, I, who had never been south of Wash-ington, D.C., had marvelous visions of the Old South slipping mysteriously into Latin America in land-scapes framed by Spanish moss.) Later, in discuss-ing "The Emperor of Ice-Cream," she explained, "In the Depression, the town was one-third Cuban, one-third black, and one-third everything else." There were labor troubles, too, she said, and the cigar fac-tories moved to Tampa. The town was full of unem-ployed cigar rollers. Cubans sold ice cream on the streets. People still used oil lamps. The poem was inspired, she maintained, by a funeral Stevens saw in Key West. Her explanation was the very antithesis of New Criticism. It was, in fact, the very stuff of apoc-rypha, but she convinced me.

She also told us in detail how Stevens went to Key West every winter with his friend and business asso-ciate Judge Arthur Powell. She even knew the hotel they stayed at—the Casa Marina. Much to our de-light, she also told us, in disapproving tones, how, in 1936, Ernest Hemingway had beaten up Wallace Ste-vens in Key West. It was, she informed us, Stevens's fault. He was drunk and had come up to Heming-way's wife (and Miss Bishop's friend), Pauline, and made an insulting comment about her clothes, which, we were further informed, "were perfectly respectable for a resort." Hemingway knocked Stevens flat. Miss Bishop spoke of the incident authoritatively and in great detail, as if she had been present. Perhaps she had. I later checked up on the incident, which seemed too colorful to be true, and found that it had really happened, though not exactly the way she described it. Stevens had actually insulted Pauline's sister, Ursula.

Miss Bishop disliked literary criticism. In 1950, she wrote for John Ciardi's anthology *Mid-Century American Poets*:

> The analysis of poetry is growing more and more pretentious and deadly. After a session with a few of the highbrow magazines one doesn't want to look at a poem for weeks, much less start writing one. . . . This does not mean that I am opposed to all close analysis and criticism. But I am opposed to making poetry monstrous or boring and proceeding to talk the very life out of it.

Twenty-five years later, her attitudes had only hardened on this subject. New Criticism was not only boring but misleading. She felt that most criticism reduced poems to ideas, and that the splendid particularity of an individual poem got lost in the process. A poem (if it was any good) could speak for itself. When she criticized the critics, she never spoke abstractly of "literary criticism," as if it were some branch of knowledge. Instead, she personalized the nemesis by referring collectively to "the critics," a sort of fumbling conspiracy of well-meaning idiots with access to printing presses. "They" were always mentioned in a kindly, disparaging way and dismissed with a single, elegant flip of her cigarette-holding hand.

Not dogmatic about her own theories, Miss Bishop did make a few exceptions: there were critics whom we were allowed to read without danger. "Allowed," however, is too weak a word, because when she liked a critic's work she liked it as intensely as the poems it talked about. Her favorite critic was her friend Randall Jarrell, who had been dead then for nearly ten years. His loss still seemed fresh, for she always spoke of him elegiacally, as if he had died only a few weeks before. Another critic she liked was Helen Vendler. She used Vendler's book *On Extended Wings*, about Stevens's longer poems, as a sort of Bible. Whenever we were to discuss one of the longer poems, she would bring Vendler's book to class. We would talk about the poem until the discussion reached an impasse, at which point Miss Bishop would suggest, "Now let's see what Vendler says." She would find chapter and verse, quote it, and only then let us go on.

I remember one rainy afternoon when a flu epidemic had decimated Cambridge. Only one other student besides me showed up for class, and the three of us sat around the table in the gloomy underworld of Kirkland House talking about "The Man with the Blue Guitar" and hearing the rain splatter against the basement windows. All of us were coughing from recent bouts with the flu, and especially Miss Bishop, who would still not stop smoking. She had, of course, brought her copy of *On Extended Wings*, and every few minutes she would stop the conversation to consult it. We would lean forward and wait for her to find the passage she wanted. Had a stranger suddenly been transported into the room, he would hardly have thought this was a seminar at Harvard University. It looked more like three old people in a rest home playing bridge with a dummy hand.

After Stevens, we moved on to Robert Lowell, and this switch gave us students an odd feeling of dislocation. Most of us were already familiar with at least some of Lowell's poetry, just as we had been with some of Stevens's and Williams's. But "Mr. Lowell," as Miss Bishop usually referred to him, was currently on the Harvard faculty. Some of us had had courses with him; all of us had met him, or, at least, heard him read his work. Miss Bishop had known him for nearly thirty years (they were introduced to each other by Randall Jarrell in 1946), and occasionally we would see them casually walking together near Harvard Square. Several of Lowell's poems were dedicated to her, and she had written the dust-jacket blurb for the first edition of *Life Studies*, reserved for us at the library. Now we were in Cambridge with her, reading Lowell's poems, living among the places and things he wrote about: the Boston Common, with Saint-

Gaudens's monument to Colonel Shaw and his black regiment; the Charles River; the towns of Salem and Concord; Copley Square and Harvard University. All this gave Lowell's work a special immediacy. And if, twenty minutes or so into class, Miss Bishop slipped, as she sometimes did, and referred to "Mr. Lowell" as "Cal" we felt a thrill of complicity, as though she were sharing some secret with us.

Such slips were not common. She tried very hard to maintain a distance in discussing Lowell's poetry. While we students reveled in her occasional reminiscences, she sensed the incompatibility of talking about Lowell as a friend and trying to discuss his poetry objectively as a teacher. Consequently, Lowell was the only poet we studied about whom she did not spend a great deal of time filling us in with biographical information. Instead, she lavished odd bits of historical, literary, and geographical information on us as we read each poem. She was particularly thorough in explaining local references in Lowell's poetry. Whenever he mentioned a Boston neighborhood or landmark, she would immediately ask how many of us had been there. Anyone who had not was given a full description plus directions on how to get there. Being a transplanted Californian, I hardly knew Boston. Soon Miss Bishop had me spending my free afternoons tramping through the Common looking for Hooker's statue and searching out the swan boats in the Public Garden. And she was right in thinking that one could learn more about Lowell's poetry by spending an hour walking around the State House than by reading an article on *Lord Weary's Castle.* The author of *North & South, Questions of Travel,* and *Geography III* took local topography seriously.

What she commented most about in Lowell's *Life Studies* was his ability to turn a phrase that summoned up a time and place. In the opening poem of the "Life Studies" sequence "My Last Afternoon with Uncle Devereux Winslow," she singled out certain phrases for special praise (my italics):

> That's how I threw cold water
> on my Mother and Father's
> *watery martini pipe dreams* at Sunday dinner.
> . . .
> my Great Aunt Sarah
> was learning *Samson and Delilah.*
> She *thundered on the keyboard of her dummy piano,*
> with gauze curtains like a boudoir table,
> . . .
> on Aunt Sarah, risen like the phoenix
> from her bed of *troublesome snacks and Tauchnitz*
>   *classics.*

Lines like these would send her off on a flurry of memories and associations, and then she would speak of *Life Studies* as if it were *her* family album. Every poem seemed like some snapshot from her childhood. She made us realize that what was so extraordinary about these poems was not that they were confessional or technically innovative but, rather, that they re-created perfectly a small world that had passed away.

Occasionally, she spoke of her own family background, but always indirectly. She never mentioned people or events—only places and things. Once, she told us about a family heirloom she had inherited—a mediocre little landscape painted by a great uncle she never knew. It was only after owning it for some time, she claimed, that she suddenly recognized the place it depicted. Decades apart, both she and her uncle had seen and been struck by the same ordinary place—a "small backwater" in Nova Scotia. She transposed this incident into her "Poem," in *Geography III*, for her poetry almost always drew its inspiration directly from life.

When we reached the end of *Life Studies*, we came to "Skunk Hour," which bears the dedication "For Elizabeth Bishop." I knew that Lowell had claimed it was partly modeled on her poem "The Armadillo," but I had always wondered if there was something else behind the dedication. (This was back in the dark ages before Ian Hamilton's biography of Lowell.) Had she figured personally in any of the episodes the poem describes? I waited for her comments—she always explained dedications to us. But this dedication she skipped over, so I decided to be bold and ask her.

"Oh, yes, it is dedicated to me, isn't it?" she said. "I really can't remember why. I'm sure he had a reason. I think it was because one summer when I was visiting him up in Castine—that's up in Maine—we heard some noises out in the backyard, and when we looked we saw a family of skunks going through the garbage. He must have remembered I was there that night."

This explanation was hardly the revelation I had hoped for, but I sat there and pretended to be satisfied. The class continued, and for once she took us firmly in hand and began a splendid reading of the poem with hardly a word or comment wasted. When she came to the sixth stanza, she talked about how cleverly Lowell worked a line from a song into the poem.

A car radio bleats,
"Love, O careless Love. . . ." I hear
my ill-spirit sob in each blood cell . . .

"Do you mean that's a real song?" someone asked.

Miss Bishop responded instantly with a look of polite horror which meant that someone had asked a stupid question. "You don't all know this song?" she asked.

We all shook our heads, and so there in the Kirkland House basement, with the pipes clanking overhead, she sang it to us in a gentle pianissimo.

Kirkland was one of Harvard's handsome neo-Georgian "river houses," situated near the Charles. The four undergraduates in the class lived in other river houses, close by, but Miss Bishop and I came from the opposite direction. Our class was so small and informal that we all left together, and unless I slipped out quickly the moment it ended, politeness dictated that Miss Bishop and I walk back toward Harvard Yard together. And politeness was a virtue nurtured in her seminar. Descending into the basement of Kirkland House after the horn-honking, shoulder-banging tumult of Harvard Square, one stepped back into a slower, more gracious world, in which no relationship was ever rushed or small courtesy hurried by. The frayed trappings of our subterranean salon, where those heating pipes were the only gilding on the ceiling and a faint smell from the rusty furnace occasionally mingled with our teacher's discreet cologne, could make this gentility seem hardwon, but here for a few hours each week decorum triumphed over decor. Each of us was addressed as "Mr." or "Miss," even the mildest expletives were deleted, and gentlemen were expected to open doors for ladies.

Unstated rules of etiquette are often the most inflexible. By holding the door for our instructor during our exodus from the Kirkland underworld, I tacitly agreed to accompany her to Harvard Yard. Likewise, I knew instinctively from the change in her voice as we rose blinking into the sober light of day that all talk of poetry was now expected to cease. At first, I thought that this sharp division between her professional and her social identities was simply another example of her unusual propriety. Not till much later did I realize how much Miss Bishop dreaded all literary conversation. Under duress, she might talk a little about poetry, but as soon as possible she would change the subject.

She once told me a story that epitomized her attitude. Northrop Frye, as the Norton Professor that year, was the guest of honor at a dinner party one night to which Miss Bishop was invited. She was embarrassed, she told me, because she hadn't read any of his books, and then was horrified to discover that she had been seated next to him at dinner. As the meal began, she leaned over to him and confessed, "I've never read any of your books." "Wonderful!" Frye replied, obviously relieved. They spent the rest of the evening chatting about Nova Scotia.

My difficulty in talking with her on our first after-class jaunts stemmed from the opposite problem. I had read all her books, and my admiration intimidated me. At first, my shyness and her formality provoked discussions mainly of a meteorological nature. Then, one afternoon, for no apparent reason (though perhaps some fortunate black cat crossed the path of my imagination), I mentioned that my mother, back in Los Angeles, was trying to breed Himalayan kittens. I was immediately besieged by detailed questions, and from that moment we never lacked for lively conversation. Our favorite topics were pets, flowers, fruit trees, church music, and travel, which usually took me to California and her, inevitably, to Brazil, where, she assured me the orchids grew even on telephone lines. On rare occasions we even talked about books. Soon we began stopping "for tea" at a nearby Russian restaurant, where we both invariably drank coffee.

As the semester progressed, the undergraduates grew openly impatient with Miss Bishop's singular ways. Their efforts at memorization became so half-hearted and their recitations so halting and resentful that in April this opprobrious requirement was quietly dropped. By then, this capitulation scarcely mattered to the unhappy few. English 285 was not the course they had hoped for, and outside class some of them had begun referring to it as "Studies in Elizabeth Bishop." One student, a bright broad-shouldered member of the Crimson football squad, summed up their despair. "I could have taken Lowell's class," he groaned. "He's going to be in all the anthologies."

Morale was not helped by the long seminar paper due in late April. We were asked to choose any modern poet (except the three discussed in class) and write an introductory essay on his or her work. In class a few weeks before the papers were due, Miss Bishop asked us which poets we had selected. No one volunteered an immediate answer, but after further questioning she learned that none of the undergraduates had made up their minds and that I had chosen Georg Trakl, a modern Austrian poet, whose work was then almost unknown in America. After some discussion, she reluctantly agreed to my unorthodox topic but not before suggesting—politely, of course—that I had squeezed this foreigner into her course through a loophole.

I knew then that I had better write a good paper. But my troubles had just begun. At the next session, all but one of the other students announced that they, too, were writing on foreign poets. Across the tiny table, I felt the cold heat of a long stare. It was the kind of look that directors call a "slow fuse"—a look like Oliver Hardy's glare the moment before he brains poor Stan Laurel and exclaims, "Here's another fine mess you've gotten us into!" More merciful than Mr. Hardy, Miss Bishop let me off with only that stare, and, hopelessly outnumbered, acquiesced in our collective xenomania, but not before asking, "What's wrong with the English language?"

Ten days after I submitted my *opus magnum* on Trakl, I received an envelope from Miss Bishop containing my essay and a typed letter. Neither the letter nor the paper's title page bore a grade. Flipping through my essay, I saw that every page had dozens of corrections, queries, deletions, and suggestions in Miss Bishop's spidery hand. Some pages had obviously been worked over three times—once in blue ink, then in red, and, finally, in the proverbial blue pencil. In horror, I began reading marginal comments like "Awful expression," "Unnecessary phrase," "A mouthful," "Not in the dictionary"—most of which were followed by an exclamation point, as was her ubiquitous and incontrovertible "No!" An occasional "Better" or "Yes" (no exclamation point) did little to revive my self-confidence. I had been weighed in the balance and found wanting. Only then did I turn to the covering letter, which began:

Dear Mr. Gioia:

You'll see that I have made many, many small marks and suggestions on your paper, but this is really because it is very good, very well-expressed, and I'd just like it to be even *better*-expressed, and, here and there, to read more smoothly.

If this was indeed a "very good" paper, I wondered, what happened to the bad ones? Then I noticed that even her own covering letter bore half a dozen revisions. Looking back over my paper, I saw that all but three of the hundreds of marks concerned questions of style. Was there a better word? Was this phrase necessary? Was I using a literary word when an everyday one would do? "When in doubt," she wrote at the bottom of one especially profound page, "use the shorter word."

By this time, I had realized that, for all her fumbling disorganization, Miss Bishop had devised—or perhaps merely improvised—a way of teaching poetry which was fundamentally different from the manner conventionally professed in American universities. She never articulated her philosophy in class, but she practiced it so consistently that it is easy—especially now, looking back—to see what she was doing. She wanted us to see poems, not ideas. Poetry was the particular way the world could be talked about only in verse, and here, as one of her fellow Canadians once said, the medium was the message. One did not interpret poetry; one experienced it. Showing us how to experience it clearly, intensely, and, above all, directly was the substance of her teaching. One did not need a sophisticated theory. One needed only intelligence, intuition, and a good dictionary. There was no subtext, only the text. A painter among Platonists, she preferred observation to analysis, and poems to poetry.

Our final examination surprised even me. A take-home test, it ran a full typed page (covered with the hand-scrawled corrections that by now were her trademark) and posed us four tasks unlike any we had ever seen on a college English exam. Furthermore, we were given exact word lengths and citation requirements, as well as this admonition as a headline: "Use only your books of poems and a dictionary; please do not consult each other."

First, the final asked us to "find, and write out, for each of our three poets, two examples of: simile, metaphor, metonymy, oxymoron, synesthesia." That seemed odd but easy. Second, we were asked to re-read Williams's "The Descent" and answer a number of questions about what particular phrases meant as well as to find parallel passages in Lowell and Stevens. Third, we were asked to "paraphrase Lowell's 'Skunk Hour' as simply as possible, first giving the *story*, what is happening in each stanza: who, when, where," and then to answer a battery of questions about particular persons, places, times, and phrases in the poem. "Be brief!" Miss Bishop had scrawled at the end of her two paragraphs of instructions for this question. These questions were unusual but not altogether unexpected, since they reflected her classroom method. It was Question No. 4 that left everyone at a loss:

> Now, please try your hand at 24 lines of original verse; three poems of eight lines each, in imitation of the three poets studied, in their styles and typical of them. (In the case of Lowell, the style of *Lord Weary's Castle*.) I don't expect these pastiches to be great poetry!—but try to imitate (or parody if you prefer) the characteristic subject-matter, meter, imagery, and rhyme (if appropriate).

We may not have consulted each other about the answers to this test, but, walking out of Kirkland after the last class with the final in our hands, we could not help talking about the questions. Miss Bishop had gone off to her office, and we were alone.

"I can't believe it," one of the undergraduates moaned. "We have to write poems."

Someone else offered the consolation that at least everything else on the exam was easy.

"Yeah, but we still have to write poems."

Later that week, turning in my final exam at Miss Bishop's office, I stopped to visit her one last time before I left for California. A student's farewell to a favorite teacher is usually a somber ritual, and I approached this occasion with the requisite melancholy. Entering her office, I wondered if I would ever see her again.

She seemed glad to see me. Indeed, she appeared generally more cheerful and carefree than I had seen her in weeks. She launched immediately into uncharacteristically lighthearted chatter, against which my youthful solemnity proved an inadequate defense. We talked for almost an hour. She even asked for my California address—that meant there would be letters. I enjoyed the visit but was slightly puzzled nonetheless. I had never seen her so animated. It was only as I rose to leave that I understood. More than any of her students, she was overjoyed that classes were over.

Remembering
Robert Fitzgerald

I

Early one afternoon in September 1976, I was at the New Haven train station, waiting to catch the Amtrak express to Boston. The weather was suffocating—a muggy Northeastern day when the sun is invisible and the morning drizzle steams from the tarmac. For two hours the public address system had assured the platform that the train would arrive in fifteen minutes. Finally I had wandered back to the terminal to fetch a cup of the "World's Finest Coffee." With my lukewarm purchase in hand, I returned through a sooty tunnel to the gate. The walls of this underworld were festive with defaced posters and lyric graffiti. Although I walked alone through the subterranean gallery, the memory of other travelers greeted me in the delicate blend of urines that filled the damp air.

Climbing the concrete stairs to the gate, I cheered myself by thinking of the friends I would visit on this last-minute trip to Boston. I had reached everyone except the person I wanted most to see, Robert Fitzgerald, who had been my favorite teacher at Harvard. I had not seen him since leaving graduate school to work in business. I hoped to talk to him about the challenges of writing poetry while holding down a full-time job. He would have practical advice. As a young man, he too had pursued his literary interests outside the academy. Knowing I would miss him on this trip, I wondered when, if ever, I would see him again.

Moist with perspiration and self-pity, I rose from the redolent stairwell into the bright haze of the platform. Just as I turned to rejoin the refugees who stood dour and defeated at the far end, I heard footsteps echoing behind me from the underpass. Glancing down, I saw an older man climbing from the shadows. Dressed despite the heat in a tweed jacket and navy blue beret, he seemed familiar, but I knew how easy it was in a new city to mistake a stranger for some old friend. Then I noticed the dark-green Harvard book bag slung over his shoulder. As I stood staring, the apparition addressed me.

"Mr. Gioia," it said in a conspiratorial whisper. "Who would have expected you?"

We shook hands and walked down the platform together. A few minutes later, without announcement, the train arrived.

"Right on time," Robert said.

I realized he thought this was the three o'clock train. I knew it was the one o'clock express, two hours late. We had been trying to catch different trains. Now boarding the same car together, we spent the next two hours having the conversation I had hoped for.

Meetings with Robert were like that. They didn't just happen. They unfolded unexpectedly, like sheer good luck. Sometimes the pure coincidence of the encounter was the amazing thing—like that tropic afternoon in New Haven. In the years that followed,

I bumped into Robert by accident in enough unlikely places—from a windswept Avenue of the Americas to a sunny Vassar quad—to make me believe in a Homeric notion of fate. But the real good fortune was the warmth of his company. I never met anyone who knew Robert—colleague, student, or competitor—who did not like him. Everyone felt he was special, not only in himself but in the qualities he brought out in those around him. Such generous unanimity is rare, especially in literary circles where personalities so often clash and jealousy flares. What made the consensus singular in Robert's case was that none of his otherwise articulate admirers, most of them writers, could explain exactly what made his company so uniquely appealing.

Conversations about Robert with his friends often came around to that question. Even intimates like William Maxwell, who knew him for half a century, ultimately declared his allure ineffable. There was his intelligence, but it wasn't just that. Neither was it his swift, understated humor nor his native gentleness and humility. There was something else—impossible to describe—hidden at the core of his personality that kept the visible gifts in perfect accord. It was that harmony that made Robert so special. I have seen many conspicuously gifted people in literary and business life—individuals of awesome intellect, boundless energy, enviable intuition—but usually the stronger the individual faculty, the more it overpowers the rest of the personality. One hears in their presence a sort of psychic dissonance. Robert's many strengths harmonized so naturally that one simply enjoyed the music of his company. Being with him, I understood for the first time how legendary pilgrims recognized their next master. A few people truly possess an aura, a tangible sense of their integrity which draws one in.

II

Good fortune played a role in how I came to know Robert, because luck, more than careful planning, led me to take two courses with him in the fall term of 1974. An unfashionable interest in prosody prompted me to enroll in "English 283: The History of English Versification," taught by Mr. Robert Fitzgerald, a name I recognized then only as the author of a Homeric translation I had not read. Meanwhile the need to work up my Latin for the doctoral language exams pushed me into an advanced course on Roman poetry whose first session proved so intimidating that I fell by default (*o felix culpa*) into the less demanding "Comparative Literature 201: Narrative Poetry," taught by the same Mr. Fitzgerald. The seminar examined the *Odyssey*, *Aeneid*, and *Inferno* with the requirement that students be able to read at least two of the poems in the original. I had just enough Latin and Italian to qualify and had already plowed through the first six books of the *Aeneid* twice in my old-fashioned Catholic high school. Comp. Lit. 201, I hoped, would be a good refresher course. It was, in retrospect, the class at Harvard that best fulfilled my fantasies of what an Ivy League seminar should be.

So daunting had the language requirement proven that only four students presented themselves on the first day in the spacious seminar room in Boylston Hall—three brilliant linguists and me. Mr. Fitzgerald, as we called him according to Harvard protocol (he did not become Robert until two years later), sat waiting for us at the head of the table. Dressed in a pinstriped suit, monogrammed shirt, and dark tie, incongruously he carried a Harvard Co-op book bag, which made him look rather like a banker who had grabbed his son's school satchel by mistake. Smoking a cigarette, he watched us settle in. Then he quizzed us on our command of Greek, Latin, and Italian. Which did we know? How long had we studied each language? What authors had we read in the original? Which translations had we used? He listened carefully to our nervous and inadequate replies.

After a long pause, he said, "Ah!, then the ancient languages are not yet entirely forgotten." Turning to the blackboard, he wrote two Latin lines from Horace and asked, "Shall we begin?"

We met twice a week each time for two hours of relaxed but learned conversation. Halfway through each session the door would open quietly, and the formidable Bette Anne Farmer, the departmental secretary, entered carrying a china tea service on a silver tray. (For a working-class Californian like me, the tea service was an exotic amazement.) Sipping tea and listening to Fitzgerald discuss the special quality of a particular line of hexameter, we experienced a combination of intelligence and humanity, scholarship and creativity, for which our previous graduate work had left us unprepared.

No Greek mariners ever succumbed more quickly to a Siren's song than we to Fitzgerald's tutelage. To our public embarrassment but private delight, he treated us as equals. (When asked by a student to sign a copy of his *Odyssey*, Fitzgerald inscribed it, "For ———, fellow student of Homer.") He was not voluble. He rarely dominated discussions. But when he talked, we listened avidly. Fitzgerald spoke slowly in a voice so intimate it seemed a whisper. Instinctively, we leaned forward to catch each word. Our anticipation was heightened by his habit of pausing between phrases, sometimes even taking a small pull of his cigarette as he formulated his exact words. In another teacher this mannerism might have become bothersome. With Fitzgerald these momentary punctuations underscored his perfect timing. He hooked the listener onto the line of his thought. Even Fitzgerald's dismissals were exact and decorous. Disagreeing with Denys Page's assertion that the *Iliad* and the *Odyssey* were written by different poets, Fitzgerald prefaced his detailed classroom rebuttal by remarking gently, "Professor Page knew more Greek at eleven than I shall *ever* learn, but here his hubris has undone him." Listening to each elegant sentence, we recognized a man who esteemed words. He exercised the same attention to his seminar conversation that he lavished on each line of poetry we studied.

Saying that Fitzgerald would linger over a particular line does not misrepresent his fastidious teaching style, which focused on specifics. He combined the classicist's devotion to unraveling, word by word, the meaning of a passage with a poet's delight in how words work together to create a memorable effect. He began each class with a line or two from the poem under discussion. He would note some narrative detail or simile we might have overlooked. By working through the passage in the original, he showed how it mirrored some aspect of the whole. Once, for example, he singled out the line in which Virgil described the serpents rising from the sea to kill Laocoön and his sons:

> *Sibila lambebant linguis vibrantibus ora.*
> (They licked with quivering tongues their hissing
>   mouths.)

After discussing the line as an example of Virgil's suggestive onomatopoeia, he also showed how it illustrated the poet's characteristic music, which came from dramatic twists of word order. Here the first word of the line, the adjective *"sibila"* ("hissing") modified the final word, the noun *"ora"* ("mouths"). By bracketing the line with these syntactic partners, Virgil adds a subtle grammatical suspense to the more obvious narrative excitement of the description. The risk in concentrating so much on textual detail is that the discrete observations never coalesce into a larger view. Fitzgerald quietly circumvented this danger with a skill that seemed effortless at the time. In retrospect, however, his apparently casual approach revealed a clear vision of how he wanted us to experience the interdependency of the three poems. What seemed like an offhand comment made one day would be picked up a few classes later with a surprising twist. A line from Homer he had paused over for its music would appear weeks later in a speech by Aeneas. A Virgilian simile he used to illustrate a strategy of Roman rhetoric would emerge almost word for word in Dante. Once, for example, he discussed an uncharacteristically epigrammatic sentence from Aeneas's speech at the fall of Troy, praising its masterfully ironic use of repetition. This way of balancing a line, Fitzgerald suggested, had influenced Ovid and other poets:

> *Una salus victis nullam sperare salutem.*
> (The one safety for the vanquished is to expect
>   no safety.)

Such pithy, end-stopped lines are rare in Virgil, and at the time this observation seemed only an interesting footnote. But when we began studying Dante, Fitzgerald started pointing out line after line that operated with similar turns. Here, for example, is the description of the Harpies attacking the souls of Suicides in Canto XIII of the *Inferno*:

> *Fanno dolore, ed al dolor finestra.*
> (They give pain and give to pain an outlet.)

Such connections are the commonplaces of philology. Usually one registers them intellectually without letting them change one's sense of the poem. By allowing us to share in the discovery, however, Fitzgerald helped us understand how poets learn specific tricks of language from their predecessors.

There was no battle between the ancients and the moderns in our class. If Fitzgerald traced the historical sources of our classic texts, he never let us forget their subsequent influence. He taught the classics as living poems. He demonstrated their vitality through unusual juxtapositions. He analyzed the rhythm in Virgil's description of Neptune riding his chariot with reference to Gerard Manley Hopkins. Likewise he suggested Virgil's powerful representation of the Trojan ships under sail, *"spumas salis aere ruebant"* (which Fitzgerald later re-created as "they plowed the whitecapped seas / with stems of cutting bronze"), illustrated Robert Graves's theory that a poet's craft comes largely from knowing how to use the letter "s." One day he asked us to read Poe's "The Philosophy of Composition," a provocative assignment for a class in the epic since the essay maintains that a long poem is a contradiction in terms. Poe famously posits that no poem can be successfully sustained for more than about 120 lines. When asked in the next session what Poe's theory had to do with Dante, Fitzgerald replied with a question. Had any of us ever counted the average number of lines of a canto in the *Inferno*? We quickly began counting. Of course, the average ran just over 120 lines.

III

If Fitzgerald believed in teaching details, he also expected us to remember them. He required us to learn every character in each poem. This assignment not only included the major figures but every soldier, shepherd, sailor, slave, or shade who appeared, even momentarily, from Aietes and Eurymedousa to Medon and Tehoklymenus—hundreds of names and characters. Though we complained at the time, in retrospect, this demand was a clever tactic to teach epic poetry. There is a temptation to read verse narrative as quickly as prose. But narrative poetry is more compressed than prose fiction, and details bear more weight. Fitzgerald slowed down our reading not only by compelling us to take careful notes but also by forcing us to differentiate Ktesippos, Agelaos, Amphimedon, Antinoos, and Eurymakhos from one another—figures we would otherwise have lumped together indiscriminately as Penelope's suitors. Fitzgerald believed that a great poet never introduced a character without good reason. Our duty was to discover and remember how each figure fit into the whole. No literature teacher had ever asked us to do a task simultaneously so simple and so comprehensive.

But then none of us had ever had a teacher who placed such paramount importance on the narrative line. My literary education had trained me to consider plotting an obvious and superficial device unworthy of serious attention. Plots were what the unenlightened noticed in literature. Showing too great an enthusiasm for the story line of a novel or long poem bordered on bad taste. Structure, symbolism, stylistics, subtext—those were the proper subjects of criticism. Now in bewilderment I watched as our instructor, Harvard's Boylston Professor of Rhetoric, discussed nuances of plot with the same care and delight with which he quoted choice lines of Greek and Latin verse.

The surface of the poem, Fitzgerald's method implied, *was* the poem. No epic survived the welter of history unless both its language and story were unforgettable. From a plot, posterity demands both immediate pleasure and enduring significance. An epic narrative must vividly and unforgettably embody the central values of a civilization—be they military valor or spiritual redemption. Only a few poets at a few fortunate points in history had met this challenge successfully. To understand the true value of these poems, Fitzgerald insisted, one not only needed to study the cultures and literary traditions that created them. One also needed to test them against life. The ultimate measure of Homer, Virgil, and Dante's greatness was that their poems taught one about life, and that life, in turn, illuminated them.

It is embarrassing to admit now that Fitzgerald's position disturbed me. In Harvard seminars one took care to avoid the four-letter word, *life*. Harvard trained us to be professional critics, and the first lesson was to keep literature separate from that sloppy, subjective category called personal experience. Sensing our skepticism, Fitzgerald borrowed a trick from Homer. He persuaded us through stories. He described how seeing Thiaki, Homer's Ithaka, had sharpened the descriptions in his translation of the *Odyssey*, as well as clarified moments in the poem. Likewise he confessed how little he had cared for the *Aeneid* until he read the poem by lamplight in a Quonset hut during the Pacific campaign. Stationed as a naval officer on battle-torn Guam preparing for the invasion of Japan, he learned to appreciate the moral weight of Virgil's concerns.

My favorite anecdote came when Fitzgerald was explaining Odysseus's special relationship to his protectress, Athena. At key moments in the *Odyssey*, the goddess visits her hero in disguise. We had just come to the episode in Book VII in which Athena appears to Odysseus as a young girl in pigtails when Fitzgerald told us about his trip to Crete to see Arthur

Evans's reconstruction of Knossos. Traveling alone and knowing no modern Greek, he had felt isolated and forlorn as he walked the streets of Heraklion. Pausing to look in a store window, he heard a voice say in English, "Good evening, sir." He turned to see a twelve-year-old girl in pigtails standing in the doorway. She had learned English, she explained, while visiting relatives in America. Their conversation cheered him immensely. As they parted, he asked her name. She responded with a common Greek appellation, "I am Athena."

Years later I heard an astronomer explain that the "simplicity and elegance" of a scientific solution represented the best criteria for its adoption. The simplicity and elegance of Fitzgerald's approach to poetry led me to question my own needlessly complicated assumptions. I realized how much my critical education had alienated me from my own experience of literature. Fitzgerald's unorthodox and often subjective remarks almost always focused on the features of the poems I found most moving and memorable. There had to be some way of reconciling one's intellectual, emotional, and moral responses to literature. "*Hoc opus, hic labor est,*" as Virgil said—"This is the trouble, there is the toil." Achieving that reconciliation would become my challenge. In the meantime, it was difficult to despair about the state of literary education while studying the classics with Fitzgerald. "Fortunate he who's made the voyage of Odysseus," wrote George Seferis. What an island of good luck it was to have spent so many afternoons with that small band in Boylston Hall.

IV

But I exaggerate. Only Tuesday and Thursday afternoons were spent in philosophic equipoise. On Monday and Wednesday I left Harvard Yard, crossed traffic-choked Massachusetts Avenue, and rode the elevator to the top of Holyoke Center, a bristling modernist high-rise designed by crossing Mies van der Rohe with a porcupine. Here, in Fitzgerald's "History of English Versification," I found a more familiar Harvard—crowded, anxious, and competitive.

On the first day the small room was jammed with students. Like me, most of the men were dressed in that fall's unofficial Harvard uniform—blue jeans, button-down shirt, and corduroy jacket. More diverse, the women displayed two sartorial varieties— preppy and *artiste*. As we waited for Fitzgerald to arrive, no one spoke, but a few glanced from face to face around the table making a dispassionate appraisal of their peers. The crowd grew. Soon students stood two deep along the back and side. I was confused. Why did so many people want to study prosody? And why did everyone look familiar? Finally, breaking the silence, I asked the fellow next to me why the specialized course was so popular.

"Don't know about them," he replied without looking at me, "but I couldn't get into English C. No connections."

"What's English C?" I asked.

"Creative writing," he replied, still looking straight ahead.

"Is that hard to get into?"

"Impossible," he explained, turning ever so slightly my way. "Unless you've got connections."

"But what does this class have to do with creative writing?"

"Don't you know?" he said—now looking straight at me with surprise, Harvard's rarest emotion.

"Know what?"

"Why everyone's here," he responded. "In this class you get to write poems."

Suddenly I realized why everyone looked so familiar—the Viking in the motorcycle jacket, the brunette with waist-length hair, the prematurely gray preppy. They made up the crowd at all the campus poetry readings. These were Harvard's aspiring *literati*.

When Fitzgerald arrived, he surveyed the mob with weary resignation. Donning a pair of black-rimmed glasses, he took out a reading list and described each of the eight books on metrics he had assigned. In addition, we needed to study the three volumes of Saintsbury's *History of English Prosody* on reserve at Widener Library. And, yes, we would also read chronologically through all five volumes of Auden and Pearson's *Poets of the English Language*. Already a few faces looked worried. The course sounded as technical as "Introduction to Particle Physics."

Turning to the blackboard, Fitzgerald then explained with many dusty chalkings and erasures his personal system for notating English scansion. Apologizing for its complexity, he reassured us how quickly we would master it through the multiple written scansions assigned for each class. There would also be a long term paper on the prosody of a classic poem. And, yes, some memorization. (A student standing near the back door quietly escaped.) Finally, he added that every week we would also be expected to write from fourteen to twenty lines of verse. Here faces brightened.

"I say 'verse,'" he explained, "because I expect nothing so exalted as poetry from these assignments. Each week I will ask you to craft a short passage according to the rules of a particular form. Do not worry about creating art. Worry only about making sense and displaying impeccable prosody." He then turned back to the blackboard and spent the next hour explaining principles of Greek and Latin metrics. By the end of the period, the board was covered with prosodic graphs and lists of terms like "hemistich" and "antepenult." There were also many lines written such as *peisteon kei meden hedu panta gar kairo kala*, which was helpfully labeled as "trochaic tetrameter catalectic."

By the time Fitzgerald dismissed us with several handouts to scan, a hundred pages of Saintsbury to read, and two verse exercises (three stanzas in strict Sapphics and fourteen lines of Catullan hendecasyllabics), the class had become less crowded. On my way out someone nudged me from the side. I turned to see a small, wiry, dark-haired fellow who looked like a spider. Not like a tarantula or anything deadly, just an ordinary spider. "Don't worry," he whispered. "He's just trying to scare us."

My interlocutor was correct. At the next session there were just enough students to fill the large seminar table. Fitzgerald's performance had frightened off the unserious. (I was not surprised to learn years later that both of his parents had been actors.) Our teacher now relaxed into a more wry and congenial presence. Although intellectually demanding, his manner was always gentle. Even his rebukes were courtly. Returning an almost illegibly faint typescript to a student one day, Fitzgerald remarked, "A young writer may not be able to change the world, but he can change his typewriter ribbon."

V

Fitzgerald's "History of English Versification" has proved so influential on certain young writers—and through them on current poetry—that it merits description. As the course title indicated, the structure was chronological. We surveyed the major metrical systems and verse forms of English poetry from

Anglo-Saxon alliterative stress meter to modernist free verse. Fitzgerald's perspective, however, was usually comparative. He examined English prosody in a European context. After presenting a passage of English poetry, he would often introduce relevant lines of Greek, Latin, French, or Italian—quotations, that is, from the foreign literatures British and American poets were likely to have known in the original.

I recently found a mimeographed handout in my folded class notebook. Titled "The English Heroic Line: A few models, analogues, examples," the sheet lists twenty-five individual lines of verse chronologically arranged from Dante (*"Mi ritrovai per una selva oscura"*) to Harvard faculty member Robert Lowell ("The Lord survives the rainbow of His will"). The first eight examples are Italian or French—roughly one-third of the total. That fraction reflects the frequency of foreign poetry in a class ostensibly on English versification. "You cannot learn to write by reading English," claimed Ezra Pound. Fitzgerald agreed. His polyglot approach demonstrated how often poetic innovation in English resulted from borrowing an established convention from Latin, French, or Italian. One language's old news becomes another's "news that stays news."

Scratch a prosodist, and you will usually find a Platonist—except with Fitzgerald. His perspective was not merely Aristotelian but Thomistic. He rarely presented abstract metrical patterns. He preferred to study actual lines of poetry. General rules were deduced from individual examples, and patterns modified to fit specific poems. Scansion played a central part in his method, but he employed it as a way of apprehending the details of the poem—a sort of auditory close reading. His approach suggested that metrical form did not meaningfully exist outside specific texts. It needed to be embodied in an actual poem.

Free verse teetotalers innocently imagine that metrics is an abstract and intellectual enterprise. For most young poets, however, studying prosody is an intoxication and debauchery, wild with verbal dance and music. Fitzgerald understood his topic's drunken appeal. If he never preached temperance, he did emphasize responsible drinking from the Pierian Spring. He cautioned us that meter was only one of several features operating in a poem. "Verse is not just meter," he observed, "but also diction, rhetoric, and syntax." Separate the elements, even for pedagogic purposes, and one risked teaching abstract simplifications. The beauty of the poetry arose from the intricate dance of its parts. The study of versification was best understood as a privileged perspective from which to consider the larger questions of poetic language.

Underlying the entire course was a profoundly Catholic sense of form as a sacramental instrument of perception. In class Fitzgerald never mentioned Jacques Maritain (though he often cited the French philosopher's two shaping influences, Aristotle and Thomas Aquinas). Maritain's neo-Thomistic ideas, however, were reflected in Fitzgerald's analytical procedures. Reviewing Maritain's *Creative Intuition in Art and Poetry* for the *Hudson Review* in 1953, Fitzgerald had spent considerable space on Maritain's exegesis of Aquinas's three requirements for beauty—*integritas* (wholeness), *consonantia* (harmony), and *claritas* (radiance). Many readers unfamiliar with theology will recognize Aquinas's famous formulation from James Joyce's *A Portrait of the Artist As a Young Man*. In his review Fitzgerald not only provides his own translation of Aquinas's definition, but goes on to a passage from Maritain that suggests his own deepest convictions:

> If we were able fully to realize the implications of the Aristotelian notion of *form*—which does not mean external form, but on the contrary, the inner ontological principle which determines things in their essences and qualities, and through which they are, and exist, and act—we would also understand the full meaning intended by the great Schoolmen when they described the radiance or clarity inherent in beauty as *splendor formae*, the splendor of the form, say *the splendor of the secrets of being radiating into intelligence.*

The italics in the final phrase are not found in Maritain's original; they were added by Fitzgerald. For him, poetic form was not an external element but an inner process coming perceptibly into being. One

79

recognized a genuine work of art by its *radiance*, the splendid clarity communicating not only its identity but its mystery. What we apprehend in art, therefore, is always greater than what we understand. Even in poetry, an art drawn from speech, most of a poem's essence remains, to use Rilke's term, "unsayable." We approach art not only with our intellect, but also with our imagination, intuition, and physical senses.

There are currently thousands of poetry-writing courses in America. Nearly all of them employ a variation of the same format—the workshop. Developed in the early twentieth century as a progressive teaching method, the workshop made group discussion of student work the focus of writing courses. Fitzgerald's teaching method bore no relation to the workshop technique. Although we wrote one or more verse exercises each week on assignment, we never discussed our work in class. At the beginning of each session, Fitzgerald would return last session's homework covered with markings penciled in his elegant, small hand. He marked any metrical mistakes or (to use his term) "infelicities." His comments were specific and usually technical. He scanned every line and syllable. "This anapest is too clumpy and blocky," he noted on one of my assignments, then followed a few lines later with "This anapest the same." He would also mention anywhere the verses failed to make literal sense. His commentary stopped there. He maintained no pretense that we were writing deathless poetry—a liberating assumption for students writing on assignment.

He insisted only that we seriously grapple with each form and handle our language responsibly.

Occasionally Fitzgerald began class by writing a student line or two on the blackboard for special praise or censure, but he never identified its author. The line was offered as an example either of a fault to avoid or a virtue to emulate. By freeing students from public evaluation of their work, he eliminated the complex group dynamics and self-esteem issues that bedevil most workshops. His focus was on the work not the workshoppers. Classroom discussion focused on classic poetry, not student poems-in-progress. Like a clockmaker taking apart an expensive time-piece, he meticulously unfolded each exemplary text so that we could see its complex but purposeful work-ings. He set our standards at the highest levels. Young writers are instinctively competitive. Fitzgerald did not deny our competitive urges. We were encouraged, however, to measure our poetic performance not against one another, but against Shakespeare, Frost, and the other classic authors of our language.

Fitzgerald also developed the only sensible system I have ever seen for grading student poems. Part of its charm was that he never explained it. In addition to his comments, each poem he returned bore a series of capital letters in the top right-hand corner. We recog-nized these abbreviations as grades, but it took a few weeks to figure out the abbreviations in his system. His grading scale—from best to worst—ran NAAB, NB, NTB, and PB. I'm happy to say I never got a PB, though I did once acquire an inglorious NTB. I only managed NAAB twice. With a candor characteristic of its creator, Fitzgerald's system concedes that the absence of badness is the proper aspiration for a student poem.

In my own case, the benefits of Fitzgerald's tutelage can hardly be overstated. When I arrived in English 283, I had been trying to write formal verse on my own for nearly six years. An autodidact may not always have a fool for a teacher, but he often has an incompetent. With the arrogance of youth, I thought I knew a great deal about prosody. In retrospect, my comprehension was undisciplined, incomplete, and approximate. Fitzgerald's rigorous but congenial approach was exactly what I needed. He quietly insisted that our work be held to the only proper standard of poetry: every word, every phrase, every line must be right. Anything less was unworthy.

If Fitzgerald's standards were rigorous, his aesthetic principles remained liberal. While insisting we master the old measures with scrupulous exactitude, he never discouraged us from working in free verse—or any other technique. He never proselytized for a single style. He advocated precision, compression, and elegance. At Stanford, where I had spent my undergraduate years, free verse and formal poets had occupied opposing camps. As a young writer who wished to work in both modes, I did not understand why one style should preclude the other. (Little did I guess then that the already incipient "Poetry

Wars" would grow more widespread and intense over the next two decades.) At Harvard, however, neither Fitzgerald nor his fellow instructor, Elizabeth Bishop, considered metrical poetry and free verse as mutually exclusive techniques. They were complementary ways of writing poetry. The important thing was to use each technique well.

Fitzgerald's taste was broad and refreshingly unfussy. To give an idea of his range of response, let me offer a few examples from a single afternoon's session. The subject was the relation of free verse technique and prose style. Fitzgerald began by quoting from three letters Gustave Flaubert sent to Louise Colet. ("A good prose sentence should be like a good line of poetry—*unchangeable*, just as rhythmic, just as sonorous.") Then he moved to Hopkins's letter to Robert Bridges on sprung rhythm. ("It is nearest to the rhythm of prose, that is the native and natural rhythm of speech. . . .") Then he quoted a passage from Shakespeare's *Henry IV, Part II* in which verse and prose were intermingled. Fitzgerald followed with some sentences from Ford Madox Ford's *The Good Soldier* that could be satisfactorily rearranged into free verse. Finally, he arrived at T. S. Eliot's "Ash Wednesday" to discuss the rhythms of syntax. Having analyzed these passages, Fitzgerald then asked us to consider the different free verse techniques of Wallace Stevens and William Carlos Williams. There was nothing narrow or doctrinaire about Fitzgerald's curriculum.

Tradition, wrote Eliot, "cannot be inherited, and if you want it you must obtain it by great labour." Fitzgerald's courses in versification and epic outlined the nature of that labor. A less abundantly gifted teacher might have minimized the effort required to master the craft of poetry. Fitzgerald painstakingly noted the challenges that existed at every level of proficiency. Twice he quoted the maxim Seneca borrowed from Hippocrates, *Ars longa, vita brevis est*. Neither Seneca nor Hippocrates, he reminded us, implied that art endures, as the phrase is so often misconstrued. Instead, the Latin meant, as Chaucer aptly translated it, "The lyf so short, the craft so long to lerne." The humane arts are immensely difficult to master. They require a life of constant application. If Fitzgerald warned us of the struggles ahead, he also showed us the multitudinous pleasures of the craft. We felt—perhaps for the first time—the kinship of artists dedicated to a common pursuit. "Sweet are the pleasures that to verse belong," wrote Keats, "And doubly sweet a brotherhood in song."

VI

I recognized at once that Fitzgerald was powerfully refining my sense of poetic craft. What I did not appreciate then, however, was the profound effect he exercised on a generation of Harvard poets. Culture depends on human energy, and there are particular moments and places where artists meet in ways that decisively shape their futures. Fitzgerald's classes in Cambridge, especially his "History of English Versification," provided one such influential nexus. (He served as the Boylston Professor from 1965 until his retirement in 1981, when he was succeeded by Seamus Heaney.) Fitzgerald became a crucial mentor to a number of the young poets who later emerged as the so-called New Formalists. No one imagined such a movement at the time, and it is unlikely that Fitzgerald intended to foster a revival of formal and narrative verse. Confessionalism and Deep Image were then the reigning fashions, and free verse was the nearly universal style. Fitzgerald was modestly famous but only as a translator of the classics. Already in his sixties, he seemed an unlikely influence on the young. Moreover, Fitzgerald's presence at Harvard—like Elizabeth Bishop's—was overshadowed by Robert Lowell, who was then America's most famous poet. Forty years later, however, the extent of Fitzgerald's influence appears a verifiable fact of literary history.

A significant number of his students—most of whom did not yet know one another—subsequently began writing in rhyme and meter. A short list of Fitzgerald students conspicuously interested in formal poetry would include Robert B. Shaw, Brad Leithauser, Mary Jo Salter, Rachel Hadas, Elise Paschen, David Rothman, and myself. Although these poets share a common fascination with form—traditional or experimental—their work is diverse in theme and scope. Fitzgerald inspired his students to explore form without imposing his own sensibility. If one adds to this core group Fitzgerald's former students who do not customarily work in meter but nonetheless demonstrate formal proclivities—poets such as Judith Baumel, April Bernard, Katha Pollitt, and Cynthia Zarin—then the flexibility of his influence becomes extraordinary. (By contrast, the formalists produced by Stanford, under the influence of Yvor Winters and his disciples, were much more stylistically uniform.) Fitzgerald's students have reflected his influence in another way. Many have designed courses on poetic form consciously modeled after the "History of English Versification." Through them Fitzgerald's ideas on prosody and poetic language reached another generation of writers. "If he was our Odysseus," one former student told me, "he had more than one Telemachus."

There is much more I could write about Robert. If I have said little about his personal life, it is because he deserves a full-length biography. His childhood was scarred by a series of family tragedies. When he was three, his mother died in childbirth. Five years later his only brother perished in the influenza pandemic. Meanwhile his father was invalided by osteomyelitis and then died when Robert was seventeen. These losses might have crippled a less valiant soul. One could also write a book about Robert's literary friendships. His intimates included Flannery O'Connor, James Agee, William Maxwell, Robert Lowell, John Berryman, Frederick Morgan, James

Laughlin, Allen Tate, Caroline Gordon, and Vachel Lindsay—not to mention his close but difficult relations with Ezra Pound.

Likewise, a proper appreciation of Robert's poetry and verse translation remains to be written. He stands as American literature's preeminent translator of classical poetry. His reputation rests not only on his celebrated versions of the *Odyssey* (1961), the *Iliad* (1974), and the *Aeneid* (1983), but equally on his powerful, stageworthy renditions of Sophocles and Euripides. From the first these translations won critical praise and earned a huge popular following. His *Odyssey* has sold nearly two million copies—making it one of the century's best-selling books of verse as well as a powerful if unacknowledged influence on later narrative poetry.

Finally, there was Robert's Catholicism, which exerted a powerful effect on many students—myself included. He was the only professor I had in eight years of college and graduate school who was a practicing Catholic. Quietly devout, he was deeply knowledgeable about Catholic intellectual tradition. His original verse occupies an important place in the history of American Catholic poetry. At Harvard he became a role model for many religious artists and intellectuals—including Jews and Protestants. I ignored all of those important topics to concentrate on the aspect of his life I knew best—his teaching of poetry.

Teaching hovers between two realities. First, there is the formal curriculum. Then there is what one really learns, which may have little to do with the syllabus. So much of what one absorbs comes neither from lesson nor lecture but from example. The way a person teaches becomes an essential part of what is taught. Robert Fitzgerald was a splendid teacher in both ways. His courses broadened my knowledge of poetry and enlarged my pleasure in the art. Meanwhile his personal presence provided an unforgettable example of a writer who was both genuinely good and deeply learned. Whenever I read Maritain's phrase, "the secrets of being radiating into intelligence," I always think of Robert and the aura of wisdom and grace he brought into class. It is a light I still learn by.

A Week with John Cheever

Photograph © Dana Gioia

I was supposed to meet John Cheever in the fall of 1974 when I was a graduate student at Harvard and a tutor at Radcliffe's North House. Among my modest academic duties was hosting a weekly literary table for undergraduates. Every Wednesday we would read work by a contemporary author and discuss it over dinner. If the arguments got lively, we would continue over drinks in the nearby apartment of our obliging faculty sponsors. The notion of a planned literary table may sound stuffy, but in practice it usually provided interesting conversations about good books. The event also gave our remote house, located almost a mile from the heart of Harvard, an excuse to invite local writers to dinner.

That fall John Cheever had begun teaching at Boston University, which had the most celebrated graduate writing program in the area. Their faculty also included Anne Sexton, John Malcolm Brinnin, and George Starbuck. I knew a young woman in the program. Whenever we met, I quizzed her about her courses and teachers, especially Cheever, whose work I had admired for years. To my surprise, she reported Cheever seemed lost and lonely in Boston. She not only suggested that I invite him to North House for dinner. She even offered to make the arrangements.

A few days later she called to confirm the time and place for Cheever's visit, adding, "Make sure you have something to drink." I immediately went out and bought three bottles of wine to ease his arrival.

A flyer announcing the visit went out to North House students, and members of the literary table were assigned "The Enormous Radio" and "The Swimmer" to prepare for the evening. I called Cheever's apartment on Bay State Road a few times to see if he needed directions. No one ever answered. "Don't worry," my friend at told me. "It's all set up."

Attendance on the night of Cheever's visit was excellent. Every regular member of the group was there plus a few new faces. One student even wore a tie. Sitting in North House's fanciest common room with three open but untasted bottles of red wine, we waited for our guest of honor. Half an hour passed. Then an hour. Finally just as the dinner service was about to close, we scooped up the bottles and rushed into the dining room to secure some food—including an extra tray for our guest, who never appeared.

I tried calling my friend to ask what had gone wrong, but I couldn't reach her. By the time we spoke a week later another event took precedence. Answering the phone, she told me that Anne Sexton had just killed herself. Anxious in the best of times, my friend was frantic and confused. Under the circumstances, Cheever's non-appearance seemed negligible. I didn't mention it. When Cheever suddenly left Boston University a few months later because of a drinking problem, it was clear what had happened on the night of our invitation.

A year later I had left Harvard's doctoral program in Comparative Literature for Stanford Business School. German, French, and English literature had been replaced by Finance, Accounting, and Statistics. Yet some things remained constant. I was still living as an advisor in an undergraduate dormitory and still running a literary table. This time, however, the project was more quixotic among the unintellectual denizens of Florence Moore Hall. "Flo Mo," as it was universally known on campus, was a dour complex of cinder-block dormitories in the postwar institutional style sometimes referred to by Californians as "early Gestapo." I was the resident advisor in Mirlo, an all-freshman dorm. I got free room and board without which I could not have afforded my graduate program.

One day in mid-January 1976 I stopped by the Flo Mo office to check my message box. The secretary told me a parent of a prospective student was coming the next day and would be staying a week in the guest room. The housemaster wanted me to show the visitor around because he was a writer.

"What's his name?" I asked without enthusiasm. She looked at her reservation card and read, "John Cheever." For a moment I forgave the housemaster his interminable staff meetings.

Intoxicated by the news of Cheever's visit, I mentioned it to some undergraduates. None of them knew who he was. Undismayed, I decided I would show them. I hurried off to the university bookstore to discover that only one of his titles was still in print. Determined to get a few books in circulation among the students before his arrival, I made the rounds of local used bookstores. One by one, I picked up about a dozen copies, including some remaindered hardcover editions of *The World of Apples*, stamped in blurry red ink on the flyleaf and priced at 99¢. I passed these books out to the more pliable freshmen with firm instructions to read the stories checked in pencil. (Such precise directions were needed since none could be trusted to read an entire volume.) Meanwhile, remembering my friend's advice from Boston, I bought some wine.

In retrospect, it is clear that January 1976 marked the nadir of Cheever's literary reputation. His last novel, *Bullet Park* (1969), had received poor reviews. *The World of Apples* (1973) had done nothing to reverse the perception of creative decline. The thin volume of stories seemed meager and uneven in comparison with Cheever's earlier collections. Worse yet, his work had stopped appearing in the *New Yorker*. Stories now surfaced at wide intervals in the *Saturday Evening Post* and *Playboy*, which were known to pay well for inferior work by famous authors.

Cheever's critical reputation had never gained the stature of his most notable contemporaries such as Updike, Bellow, Roth, Mailer, or Ellison. The short story may be America's greatest contribution to world literature, but as a genre, it does not carry the cultural prestige of the novel. The popular success of Cheever's stories during the postwar years made him an easy establishment target in the late sixties. He had never attracted much serious critical attention, but now his work was not so much discussed as glibly dismissed as dated suburban satire. He had become the ceremonial scapegoat for all the real and imagined sins of the *New Yorker*. He was still credited with a few classic stories of middle-class angst. They were permanent features in the anthologies. His novels, however, were considered messy amalgamations of short narratives.

Literary celebrity is ephemeral. Without the support of critics and with little new work to attract notice, Cheever had lost the younger generation of readers. They were reading his contemporaries or juniors. Even if new readers wanted explore his work, it would have been difficult since it was mostly out of print. Nowhere was his reputation lower than among the radical chic of Northern California who did not spare him their most obscene epithets—elitist, Eastern, suburban, and (lips tightening to a sneer) middle class.

The next morning the house secretary phoned to say that Mr. Cheever had arrived. She asked me to go over and show him the campus. Then she added in a quiet tone, which seemed to bespeak all of history's lost causes, "He wants to eat in the dorm." Here indeed was a man in need of guidance

The Florence Moore guest room was a small concrete-block cubicle set on ground level at the end of a dormitory hallway. Rarely used except by visiting parents in distress or relatives of foreign students who didn't know better, its stark walls and low ceiling contained a steel bed, a small desk, a dresser and a closet-sized bathroom. Everything but the furniture was painted a pale institutional green.

Not surprisingly, Cheever was pleased to see me. I apologized for the room, but he immediately replied, with the chivalrous generosity which would characterize his stay, that it was absolutely perfect. The room had a desk and windows, he pointed out, as if these were rare appurtenances in the world of accommodations. He did not mention that his ground level windows looked out to the student bicycle racks. His compliments seemed so sincere that I felt I had done that obviously splendid suite an injustice.

Although Cheever looked exactly like his dust jacket photographs, three things surprised me. First, he was so small. For some reason, probably connected with my mental images of his fictional protagonists, I had expected a magisterially tall Yankee gentleman. Instead I met a slight, boyish man who stood only a few inches over five feet. Second, Cheever was the most perfectly poised man I had ever met. Every gesture was so graceful that he scarcely seemed part of the clumsy everyday world. Even the way he sat still seemed as carefully composed as a portrait. Not that his presence was dramatic; just the opposite was true. His manner was relaxed and understated. Nevertheless he had a style that captivated one's attention the way a great actor can steal a scene without speaking a word. Finally, I was stunned by his voice.

Cheever spoke a brand of patrician Massachusetts English that I now suspect he invented, for I have never heard anyone else speak quite like it. Nevertheless, he used this suave, fictive dialect so convincingly that in his voice it carried the force of ancient authority. I had talked to men funnier or wiser than Cheever, more inventive or intelligent, more perceptive or likeable, but I had never met anyone who possessed all these qualities so generously in such deft balance. His wasn't the pedestrian balance of an earnest earthbound mind but the equilibrium of an acrobat.

Cheever's conversation was the natural extension of his physical poise. He never said anything merely for effect, but everything he said was phrased effectively. There wasn't anything pretentious about his conversation, but he would add some small detail of language or delivery to his sentences that made them seem just ever so slightly remarkable. He also paid attention to his listeners. One had the feeling he watched his listener's every response and tailored even the oldest story to the special requirements of the occasion. The Flo Mo freshmen, who did not care much about literature (or most adults), appreciated this attention. It was one reason why they joined him at meals whereas usually they dreaded sitting with visiting faculty. His conversation never excluded them. His intelligence was enlivening. And he was very funny. As he remarked, "You can't expect to communicate with anyone if you're a bore."

We talked in the guest room while Cheever waited for his son Fred (or Federico to give his full Christian name, which his father enjoyed using). They had arrived together, but Fred had vanished after delivering his father to Flo Mo. He had gone to stay with friends from Andover elsewhere on campus.

The ostensible object of Cheever's visit to Stanford was to see what kind of school it would be for his son. Indeed, both as we waited that morning and over the next week, he quizzed me repeatedly about the school, the faculty, the area, even the sports teams. Likewise he enjoyed discussing the relative merits of Stanford versus other schools with the Flo Mo freshmen who were delighted to be treated as authorities on the subject. I couldn't help thinking that these efforts were done more for himself than Fred. He talked constantly about his son but in an oddly formal way for a father. He played the role of the attentive father—especially around the freshmen—but his performance had a certain studied air that suggested the sincere effort of a man who had difficulty in showing his love for his children.

When Fred finally appeared, it was obvious the prospective student needed no paternal assistance in sizing up Stanford. Having made sure that his father was safely ensconced at Flo Mo, he quickly left to rejoin his Andover friends with whom he spent the rest of the week. I saw father and son together again only once before they returned East. Neither seemed to mind the separation.

Fred looked a great deal like his father, though he was taller and slightly more handsome. Their resemblance was accentuated because both father and son were dressed identically in the prevailing preppy style—tweed sports coat, crew neck sweater over a long-sleeved shirt, slacks, and penny loafers. While such haberdashery was not remarkable for Fred, who, after all, was a preppy, it was less common for a sixty-three-year-old man. Yet Cheever's clothes suited him. He had never bothered to grow old. He still seemed more bright young man than sagacious patriarch. No one who met him that week would have guessed his full age.

As his staff host, I expected to see little of Cheever after taking him to lunch the first day. To my astonishment, I spent most of the next week with him. He had arrived at Stanford with the best of intentions but the vaguest of plans. Since Fred was busy following his friends, his father had nothing to do except wait several days for a hastily arranged class visit and public reading. Cheever knew no one at Stanford, and the people who might have sought him out were mostly unaware he was on campus. He accepted his idleness and neglect without comment.

For the next few days, Cheever just hung around Flo Mo, treating this large, spider-shaped complex like a resort hotel. He lingered over meals until the last student left and then sat in one of the run-down and usually deserted lounges. Whenever I returned from classes, I would find him sitting by himself smoking in one of the huge Naugahyde chairs. He agreed to almost any suggestion I made—a walk, a drive, a visit. Eventually I gave him a key to my room so he could borrow books or listen to records when I was in class.

It is impossible to summarize that week of conversations, spoken in dining halls against the clatter of trays and silverware, on meandering walks through the wooded campus, in an old car winding through green January hills to the Pacific. Now, years later, the exact words are lost—like Stanford's bulldozed woodlands—and with Cheever the exact words were always much of the magic. Still, a few things have stuck with me, though what I remember is not what was said but that part of it which I was prepared to hear. These fragments do scant justice to the man they try to evoke.

So much about Cheever surprised me. First, I remember his modesty as a writer. He did not lack self-esteem, but it was tempered by his recognition of the immensity of the writer's task. Having already met a few self-absorbed literary mediocrities, I found John's humility before his vocation pure and unaffected. It was a kind of innocence. He was proud of what he had written but without pretension. He appeared unconcerned with posterity, which he claimed would take no note of him. What he valued was his relationship with his audience. He repeatedly mentioned the letters he received from the *New Yorker* readers, those "estimable men and women," who wrote to say how much they enjoyed reading one of his stories. What mattered was literature as an act of shared discovery between the writer and the reader. Fiction, he insisted, was innovative not by technical experimentation but by being "constantly and profoundly questioning."

I was also intrigued by John's candid conversations about his own religious impulses. He told me he went to church and communion on Sunday morning, sitting quietly for the better part of an hour, because this was one place where he could become spiritually refreshed. He believed in God, he insisted, but in an evanescent way impossible to describe to anyone else. Despite his high Episcopalian churchgoing, he seemed less Christian than deist. Religion also had an important social and cultural function for him. In his own unorthodox way, he celebrated the Communion of the Saints; churchgoing affirmed his connection with other people—both living and dead. It was a means of keeping faith with the past. For that reason he only felt comfortable with traditional liturgy. He praised Thomas Cranmer, *The Book of Common Prayer*, and even the Latin Mass. Like literature, liturgy was a great language that linked the past and present.

Cheever's spiritual sense was inseparable from his vocation as a writer, though critics have rarely noticed this connection. He was not primarily a satirist of suburban manners but an essentially religious writer. Despite the detailed realistic settings, his stories are often parables. The underlying narrative takes the form of a pilgrimage in which the protagonist, shaken by some unexpected turn of events, searches out the meaning of his or her existence. These sudden and sometimes involuntary journeys inevitably strip away the delusions—gentle or grievous—from the self-images of Cheever's characters. Humbled or humiliated, they face their own finitude in relation to the infinitely luminous natural world around them. Cheever's theme was not mores but mortality, and his mode lyric rather than satiric. His vision was metaphysical with a heightened sensitivity of the spiritual, like shadows cast by the light of the physical world. Was it the unusual surface brilliance of Cheever's work that so often fixated critics on its most literal level?

Finally, I was struck by John's belief that a real writer could and indeed should lead an ordinary life. Genius didn't need to be rootless, disenfranchised, or alienated. A writer could have a family and a job. A writer could even live in a suburb. His marriage, children, home, all the ordinary elements of everyday life, were immensely important to him. Talking about them, he proselytized in a way he never did about religion. I could feel his passionate concern for these modest human values. Indeed I was dazzled by his talk which could make a mortgage or a report card shimmer like sacred script. In retrospect, given what we now know about Cheever's personal failings, his craving and esteem for these primal human connections has a tragic quality. I did not realize then how bitterly and briefly won these quotidian consolations had been for him. I did, however, sense that I had encountered him at a singular moment of his life when he had been both chastened and renewed by his confinement in an alcoholic rehabilitation center.

Cheever's insistence on viewing the writer as a whole person colored his judgments on the authors he had known. We talked, no doubt at my eager prompting, about his famous literary friends—Edmund Wilson, John Dos Passos, James Agee, Malcolm Cowley, Saul Bellow, John Updike, and others. The writer he spoke of most fondly was E. E. Cummings, who had been a literary foster-father for him in his early New York days. Cummings's vitality, intelligence, and dedication made a profound impression on Cheever. Estlin had become the model for the kind of writer Cheever wanted to be. (How astonished I was back then to hear writers referred to by their first names!) Later that week he summed up Cummings's importance in a Cheeveresque way, saying that the poet made it clear "that one could be a writer and also remain highly intelligent, totally independent, and be married to one of the most beautiful women in the world."

I also remember little things Cheever said. Talking about some fine point of prose style, he announced, "I have never used italics. Never! If I am tempted to underline my meaning in that crude way, I go back instead and revise the sentence." At once I began noticing how superfluous and heavy-handed italics were—a vulgar typographical trick. I revised them out of my own prose. When one crept in despite my vigilance, I blushed to see it in print. Surely the audience recognized the blunder as a sign of poor literary breeding. I was relieved years later when in one paragraph of a Cheever sketch I came across three italicized words. Granted, it was an uncollected piece, but it comforted me to know that even Homer nods. The discovery gave me permission to italicize the *occasional* word.

During this week at Stanford Cheever had a particular radiance that he had already lost by the time I next saw him two years later. He exuded the aura of joy and serenity that people acquire after a religious conversion or recovery from deadly illness. Cheever had been resurrected from the dead. Having been rescued from alcoholism, he had begun a new life. When I offered him some wine the first night, he spoke at length about his alcoholic collapse and subsequent treatment in the Smithers Rehabilitation unit in Manhattan. I was embarrassed by his candor. His calm but lurid confessions were not what I had expected from a famous author. He described shameful episodes of drunkenness and spoke of his treatment with gratitude. I realized that his victory over alcohol was the basis of his present happiness. Only a few months out of an alcoholic rehabilitation center, he had no romantic delusions that drinking was fate's price for his poetic soul. Alcohol was a destructive addiction he had painfully overcome.

The night of his public reading some of the freshmen decided to take John out to dinner. We chose a modest French restaurant in Menlo Park, and a dozen of us came along. My high school friend, Jim Laffan, who had first introduced me to Cheever's work, drove down from San Francisco. Delighted that the waiter didn't ask for I.D.'s, the freshmen all ordered wine. They kept offering it to John who smiled, sipped his club soda, and smoked. He entertained us with stories about teaching creative writing at Boston University and Sing Sing. He claimed that his students at Sing Sing had shown more aptitude. At the end of the meal as the freshmen searched drunkenly through their wallets, several discovered they didn't have enough money to pay their share of dinner. With consummate politeness John quickly took the bill, counted the inadequate cash at hand, and made up the difference from his own pocket, refusing to let either my friend or me chip in more than our share. Not only did John not mind the embarrassing situation, he enjoyed being cast in the role of the parent getting his kids out of a jam.

Cheever had not been formally invited to read at Stanford. He had been asked only after the English faculty learned he was coming to campus with his son. Scheduled at short notice, the reading took place in Bishop Auditorium at the Graduate School of

Business, the same room my Finance class had met in that morning. It was the only empty hall on campus. In the car from the restaurant, John began coughing violently. Arriving at the Business School, we found him a water fountain, but it barely helped. "This isn't nerves," he told us firmly.

The auditorium was full with about two hundred people, almost all middle-aged or older. Few students had come and only a handful of the English faculty. John was introduced by Richard Scowcroft, the head of the Creative Writing Program. He was visibly excited by Cheever's visit. While his guest of honor hacked away beside him, Scowcroft gave a warm and nostalgic introduction about reading Cheever's stories as a young man. The elegiac tone of Scowcroft's remarks betrayed the tacit assumption—probably shared by most of the audience—that Cheever was now at the end of his career.

John appeared to improvise his program, but actually his first two selections that evening were a set program from which I never subsequently heard him depart. He began with "The Death of Justina," one of his best but least celebrated stories, followed by "The Swimmer," which he introduced with anecdotes about its filming in Hollywood. He ended with a brief sketch he called "The Death of the Short Story." (It was actually the conclusion to "A Miscellany of Characters That Will Not Appear.") This witty but slight excerpt suffered in comparison with its two bewitching predecessors.

Cheever began badly. He coughed his way through "Justina," chopping it to bits. His sudden frailty gave his exquisite prose a special poignancy.

On Saturday the doctor told me to stop smoking and drinking and I did. I won't go into the commonplace symptoms of withdrawal but I would like to point out that, standing at my window in the evening, watching the brilliant afterlight and the spread of darkness, I felt, through the lack of these humble stimulants, the force of some primitive memory in which the coming of night with its stars and its moon was apocalyptic. I thought suddenly of the neglected graves of my three brothers on the mountainside and that death is a loneliness much crueler than any loneliness hinted at in life. The soul (I thought) does not leave the body but lingers with it through every degrading stage of decomposition and neglect, through heat, through cold, through the long winter nights when no one comes with a wreath or a plant and no one says a prayer.

Very slowly his throat cleared. By the time he reached "The Swimmer" his suave storyteller's voice had returned. For the next twenty minutes the audience was mesmerized. Hearing this famous story again, they knew it was a small masterpiece. The spell, however, was quickly broken by the brittle humor of his concluding sketch which seemed small and cold by comparison. Though it was an old piece, he did not introduce it as such. Its minor elegance seemed to confirm rumors of his recent decline. To make matters worse, he began rushing through the text, perhaps sensing that it was not coming across well. As he finished, the audience applauded generously.

We left our celebrated author to manage the Creative Writing Department's reception on his own. Outside on the Business School steps I noticed one of the junior professors smoking a cigarette. He was telling an undergraduate that Cheever's talent was exhausted and his career was over. Two years later Cheever published his novel *Falconer*, to ecstatic reviews. His photo appeared on the cover of *Newsweek* with the caption "A Great American Novel," as the book climbed to the top of the best-seller list. The following year, *The Stories of John Cheever* also reached the best-seller list before winning the Pulitzer Prize, National Book Award, and National Book Critics Circle Award.

Cheever's reading was his one public moment at Stanford. Earlier in the week he had had little opportunity to enjoy the special status of a visiting literary celebrity because his arrival had been upstaged by another last-minute visitor, Saul Bellow. Bellow's unexpected sojourn had also been occasioned by family business. His new wife was interviewing in the Mathematics Department. He had accompanied her to tease the University with the prospect of a package deal. The Administration exhibited no hesitation in swallowing the bait.

If Cheever's literary star was in decline, Bellow's was indisputably ascendant. His last novel, *Mr. Sammler's Planet* (1970), had won the National Book Award making him the first and only author ever to win that eminent prize three times. His new book, *Humboldt's Gift* (1975), which would win him a second Pulitzer Prize, had been rapturously received. Bellow's photograph had recently smiled from the cover of several national magazines. Moreover, he was widely—and, as it happened, correctly—rumored to be in consideration for a Nobel Prize. An author who never cultivated publicity in the ostentatious manner of his contemporaries such as Truman Capote or Norman Mailer, Bellow had become an international celebrity. The English Department and the Administration waxed ecstatic. The former saw a classic author, the latter a classy acquisition.

One reason Cheever was ignored during most of his stay was that his hosts were busy courting Bellow. Cheever neither begrudged nor envied Bellow his royal reception. It was obvious, even to an outsider, that like Queen Elizabeth's endless inspections of expanded hospital wings and improved bridge crossings, Bellow's tour offered little enjoyment to the visiting monarch. The Administration had crammed the novelist's short stay with meetings, parties, speeches, and public appearances.

Bellow bridled at some of the more ludicrous engagements such as speaking in a dormitory to a restless group of students who only vaguely knew who he was. Yet he followed his official schedule with a weary air of obligation. He deceived no one, however, into thinking he was enjoying himself. Administrators wrung their hands. Cheever, half diplomat and half palace gossip, quietly pointed out each academic faux pas and embarrassment.

Bellow certainly looked regal. Although, like Cheever, he was very short and poised, their similarity ended there. John seemed amiably relaxed and informal. Bellow projected unapproachable dignity and reserve. He entered a room with intimidating confidence. At sixty he was still trim and handsome. His well-tanned skin was unwrinkled, his thin grey hair brushed into deceptive thickness. A king's haberdashery would not have surpassed his wardrobe. His tight tailored suits and hand-sewn shirts stood in splendid isolation from the academic crowd of crumpled tweed and corduroy.

On his last evening Bellow agreed to give a short reading, but he requested that Stanford allow no publicity. To keep the event small, he also required the reading be held in a student residence. Anxious to end his difficult visit nicely, the Administration prefaced the reading with a fancy cocktail party and dinner.

By happy coincidence, the reading was planned for Mirlo, the section of Florence Moore Hall where I served as resident advisor. For this reason I was invited to the preliminary festivities. It was my first literary cocktail party.

Being young and callow, I assumed that writers enjoyed talking with strangers about literature. After all, I did. At the packed party, while Wallace Stegner chatted with Donald Davie and Cheever caught up with Bruce Bliven, I tried to engage Bellow in literary conversation. He winced at each of my eager questions before making a pointedly terse reply. Posterity, alas, will be denied a complete record of our *tête-à-tête* because I have blocked out all but one of the exchanges made before I slinked off in defeat. I only remember asking what contemporary fiction Bellow most admired. "Literature is not a competitive sport," he replied curtly. Unaware I had asked for a game score, I was about to apologize, but suddenly he rattled off what I assume was the first-inning batting order for his own literary All-Stars Game: "Wright Morris, J. F. Powers, and a man standing in this room," he paused for effect, ". . . John Cheever."

It struck me as significant even then that Bellow did not praise any of the authors critics would have considered his rivals—Updike, Roth, Ellison, and Mailer—but his admiration for Cheever was genuine. Bellow's esteem was returned by Cheever who viewed him as his most gifted contemporary. But while Cheever respected Bellow's writing, he was not above gossiping about the novelist's life. He would entertain me with extraordinary stories about Bellow's life in Chicago and New York. At the cocktail party he assured me *sotto voce* that Bellow was considering a job at Stanford mainly to get away from his ex-wife in Chicago. As he described the unusual ways this prodigious harridan plagued her ex-husband, I began to wonder if all of John's deliciously detailed stories were true.

After dinner our group wandered into the Mirlo lounge which was already filling up. Cheever and I grabbed front row seats. I noticed then that Bellow was carrying neither a book nor manuscript. A few minutes before the reading was to begin he walked over to his host, the Director of Residential Education, and declared, "I need a copy of *Humboldt's Gift.*"

The director turned pale. How could he find a copy of a new novel available only in hardcover in a freshman dorm? He rushed off to search the audience for a copy. Overhearing the conversation, I sprinted to my room to retrieve what was probably the only *Humboldt's Gift* within half a mile (which I possessed only by accident). Just as the director was returning to Bellow after having frantically petitioned the crowd in vain, I handed the author his new novel. Bellow accepted it without a word.

The hall was now overflowing. Seeing two elderly women desperately eyeing the packed room, John got up and led them with great panache over to our seats. We then sat on the floor in front of them. Bellow walked over to us, bent down, and said, "John, you'll pardon me if I make a fool of myself, won't you?"

With Cheever's advance absolution, Bellow walked up to the microphones and began a powerful reading of two long passages from *Humboldt's Gift*. Making almost no introductory comments, he plunged into the heart of his intricate *roman à clef* about his turbulent friendship with the poet Delmore Schwartz. Most of the audience was soon lost, but to the few who had read the book, his fluent reading was intellectually and emotionally dazzling. Or at least the sound of his voice was. The audience could barely see the diminutive man behind the three large microphones placed to amplify and record the event. Cheever leaned over to me and whispered, "I can hear Saul, but all I see are a shiny pair of reading glasses peeking over the microphones."

Finishing the second passage, Bellow looked up and snapped the book shut. The audience exploded in applause. Smiling stiffly, he quickly walked in front of the microphones and nodded in place of a bow. The moment the applause ceased, he held out the book. Since he wasn't looking at me, I didn't immediately realize that this was my signal to fetch the volume, but I stood up and retrieved it. By then people were crowding to the front of the room to meet the author. Bellow was too quick for them. As soon as I took the novel from his outstretched hand, he disappeared out the side door. Thus ended Saul Bellow's visit to Stanford.

On his last day Cheever agreed to sit for an interview to be published in *Sequoia*, the Stanford literary magazine. I drove him up through Stanford's sumptuous "faculty ghetto" to the house of Virgil Whitaker, the Elizabethan scholar, who had loaned us his

living room. Michael Stillman, who had recorded
Bellow and Cheever all week, set up his equipment in
the huge glass walled room which commanded a 120°
hilltop view of the Stanford campus and nearby foot-
hills. Millicent Dillon, who free-lanced for the Stanford News and Publication Service, asked if she could
join us. We invited her along.

Most of Cheever's published interviews reflect his
uneasy and defensive attitude towards critics (among
whom he counted interviewers). He usually viewed
his interlocutor competitively. His answers could be
sharp and aggressive. Determined not to be misunder-
stood, he often rejected, redefined, or even ridiculed
questions until the embattled interviewer offered a
new query worthy of serious response.

By comparison, our long afternoon conversation
with Cheever was relaxed and amiable. Perhaps the
unusual situation of having three interlocutors made
the occasion seem more like a social conversation
than an individual duel. He took an immediate liking
to Mike and Millicent. After a few preliminary pleas-
antries, he leaned back on the large couch and talked
for nearly three hours. When the conversation eventually appeared in *Sequoia*, Cheever wrote, "I thought
the interview splendid." He claimed it was the only
successful taped interview he had ever done. I suspect he was pleased at the way the interview caught
the fanciful quality of his conversation.

The published version of the interview, however,
contained only a fraction of the conversation. The

editor cut thirty-five single-spaced pages of transcript down to the six published pages. At least as much interesting material vanished as finally appeared. The full transcript was then discarded, but years later I recovered the original tape, transcribed, and published it—with only Cheever's "off the record" comments omitted. Some of John's best remarks therefore disappeared by prior agreement. Several times during the interview he told us he was speaking "off the record." Some of these private remarks concerned his experiences in the Soviet Union. He did not want his words to jeopardize any of his Soviet acquaintances. There were also some devastating appraisals of a few contemporaries. For example, Cheever described one celebrated novelist by saying, "his principal gift was the ability to describe bilge water, rotting wood, and the smell of wet hemp."

At the end of the interview I drove him back to his room. We talked a few minutes. Then Fred arrived. They had to leave for the airport, so we made our quick farewells.

We exchanged a few short letters. After moving to New York in 1977 I occasionally saw Cheever at readings, but I never pursued our friendship. The week at Stanford had been a special situation that one could not repeat. By that time, too, not only had he recouped his critical fortunes with *Falconer*, but he had also achieved a greater public celebrity than ever before. This success made me reluctant to presume on his earlier generosity. I felt more comfortable seeing him beaming from the cover of *Newsweek* or chatting on television with Dick Cavett.

The last time I saw John was by accident. In late September 1981 my wife and I went to hear Eudora Welty speak at the Katonah Library. It was a crisp autumn day when the leaves in Westchester were just beginning to turn, the sort of day Cheever so frequently celebrated in his work. Outside the library a long, noisy line of people waited for the doors to open. Walking to the end of the line, we passed Robert Penn Warren, William Maxwell, and Robert Fitzgerald. Everyone seemed hale and happy. A waterfall of conversations filled the air.

Then I saw John and his wife Mary standing quietly near the end of the line. He looked thin, ashen, and painfully frail next to her. When he coughed, he shook with pain. That afternoon John seemed decades older than the quick, boyish man I had met six years before. I stopped to say hello, but as we talked, he sounded so tired that I quickly excused myself. After the reading Mary led him gently through the packed room towards the door. I watched them over the bobbing heads of the crowd until his tiny, shuffling frame disappeared into the early evening.

"How Nice to Meet You, Mr. Dickey"

Photograph © South Carolina ETV

You don't always meet the authors you admire under the best possible circumstances. Human encounters—like most other natural phenomena—occur in random patterns that range from best to worst. In 1987 I met James Dickey under uncomfortable circumstances. I tried to make the best of a bad situation. He insisted on making the worst of it. At the time I was surprised, though not particularly offended, by his behavior. In retrospect, I think he may have had the right idea—at least for an artist. If you are going to have a disaster, why not conduct it in the grand style? My encounter taught me something about life: it is often better not to meet the writers you admire.

Why not take that maxim one step further? Perhaps it is best not even to review the writers you admire. As any regular reviewer learns, you don't always get assigned the right books by your favorite authors. Sometimes you get a stinker. Then you have only three choices—none of them attractive. You can send the book back to the editor with an excuse. You can lie. Or—worst of all—you can tell the truth.

My first and best encounter with James Dickey was on the page. It happened in 1971. I was at Stanford in the Junior English Honors Seminar. Our professor was Diane Wood Middlebrook, who twenty years later would achieve literary celebrity as the biographer of Anne Sexton. Middlebrook was brilliant, charismatic, and quite glamorous. She seemed less like an English professor than a movie star playing an English professor. She wore miniskirts. She held class on the lawn under an oak tree. She let students smoke. The male students were all slightly in love with her, and so were a few of the women. This was California in the seventies. "Bliss was it then to be alive," as Wordsworth wrote of an earlier revolution, "but to be young was very heaven."

The purpose of the class was to develop our critical skills by carefully studying major literary texts. Middlebrook assigned the work of only three poets. Two of them were dead—Wallace Stevens and Theodore Roethke. Middlebrook was writing a book about Stevens and had studied with Roethke. One of our major poets, however, was alive. Indeed he was still in mid-career—James Dickey.

We were assigned Dickey's early collected volume, *Poems: 1957–1967*, which had recently appeared in paperback. I studied the green, glossy covered book from front to back. Certain poems captivated my imagination—"The Lifeguard," "The Heaven of Animals," "The Scarred Girl," and "The Sheep Child." Their visceral power and originality expanded my sense of contemporary poetry. I was also intrigued by his sprawling and disorderly longer narratives, "Falling" and "The Firebombing." (Years later, the *New Yorker*'s poetry editor, Howard Moss, told me that "Falling" had generated more mail than any other poem he had published in the magazine.) Dickey became for me one of the important poets of his generation. Even then, however, I noticed how uneven his work was. The successful poems were few and far between.

In 1971 Dickey seemed like an author working at the height of his powers. Both a poet and novelist, he was proclaimed as the voice of the New South—the successor to William Faulkner, Robert Penn Warren, and Flannery O'Connor. A year earlier he had published his best-selling novel *Deliverance*, which was already headed for Hollywood. Dickey demonstrated the possibilities for fame and success that still seemed open to American poets. Robert Lowell, Anne Sexton, Allen Ginsberg, and posthumously Sylvia Plath were cultural celebrities then—in a way that few estimable American poets are today. Vigorous, outspoken, and unabashed, Dickey appeared a writer of boundless energy. Who then could have imagined that his poetic career was essentially over? Or predict that his first selected volume—consisting entirely of poems published in a single decade—would contain virtually all of his enduring work?

Over the next decade I continued to reread his early poems. At one point I even wrote Dickey (and several other writers) to solicit biographical information for my essay "Business and Poetry." I paid his new work no special attention, however, until 1982, when I was assigned a "Poetry Chronicle" for the *Hudson Review*. As the books arrived for consideration, I was cheered to see *Puella*, a new volume by Dickey. I selected it for review.

I read *Puella* with dismay. The new collection was not merely weak. It was awful. Usually when a strong author writes an inferior book, some glimmer of talent remains. A fan, therefore, may harbor a not unreasonable affection for a flawed performance. I feel this way about spotty but interesting works such as F. Scott Fitzgerald's *Pat Hobby Stories*, Tennessee Williams's *The Milk Train Doesn't Stop Here Anymore*, and Anne Sexton's *Transformations*—all fascinating messes. Not so with *Puella*. Here was no estimable endeavor only half realized in performance. It was a total rout, a ship gone down with all hands aboard.

Dickey had notable strengths as a poet—narrative skill, realistic description, and an instinct for sensational and disturbing subject matter. There was no surprise when Dickey published his gritty and violent novel *Deliverance*. He had the compelling voice of a Southern storyteller. What Dickey lacked as a poet, however, was equally notable. He had no special gift for lyric language. The strength of his lines was rhetorical rather than musical.

Puella consisted of eighteen interconnected love poems written in a high lyric style linked loosely in an associative structure. The basic concept seemed perversely chosen to exploit Dickey's weaknesses and ignore his strengths. The poems sprawled and drooped with sublime indifference to sense or substance. *Puella* was Pat Boone singing Heavy Metal,

Roseanne doing a love scene in the nude, Mick Jagger starring in *The Music Man*. It was so bad I knew it would win a prize. And, of course, it did.

Even at his best, Dickey is difficult to quote convincingly. He is expansive. His power comes from the total effect of the work rather than in stunning individual lines. What animates his poems is their originality of subject and the strength of the narrative. Here is the opening of "The Heaven of Animals," an early poem which presents a fascinating premise— the nature of a non-human paradise—in everyday language, just slightly heightened by repetition and parallel syntax. Notice how quickly the Edenic opening lines modulate into Darwinian violence, a characteristic move for Dickey:

> Here they are. The soft eyes open.
> If they have lived in a wood
> It is a wood.
> If they have lived on plains
> It is grass rolling
> Under their feet forever.
>
> Having no souls, they have come,
> Anyway, beyond their knowing.
> Their instincts wholly bloom
> And they rise.
> The soft eyes open.
>
> To match them, the landscape flowers,
> Outdoing, desperately

Outdoing what is required:
The richest wood,
The deepest field.

For some of these,
It could not be the place
It is, without blood.
These hunt, as they have done,
But with claws and teeth grown perfect,

By contrast, the poems in *Puella* reached for exquisite lyricism in a High Modernist mode, a style that requires verbal music, evocative diction, powerful imagery, and genius for indirect associative meaning. It is impossible to describe the particular awfulness of *Puella*; one can only quote. Here are the opening lines of "Veer-Voices: Two Sisters Under Crows" (a title that already suggests the problems to come).

Sometimes are living those who have been seen
Together   those farthest leaning
With some dark birds and fielded
Below them   countercrying and hawing in savage openness
For every reason.   Such are as we, to come out
And under and balance-cruise,

Cross-slanting and making long, raw, exhaustless
Secret-ballot assertions   feeding and self-
supporting our surround

By all angles of outcry; it seems to lift and steady us
To the ground.

What was one to make of this passage? The question is not just whether the lines were written by a native speaker of English, but whether they were written by a human being. They sound like an unfortunate early experiment in artificial intelligence.

"Veer-Voices: Two Sisters Under Crows" was not a momentary lapse in an otherwise passably good collection. It was typical of Dickey's misguided enterprise. He sought to create a sublime style in which the music and imagery achieve intense lyricality. What resulted was a verbal bulletin board on which isolated phrases and images are pinned in accidental order. Here is the opening of "Deborah in Mount Sound: Bell, Glacier, Rose" (even the title is a bulletin board):

> Averaging-sound
>
> Of space-thinning   space-harvesting metal—
>
> Obsessional, the outstaying
> Life-longing intervals, wherein,
>
> Reasonless as cloud, the male's one luminosity
>   is frozen
>
> In a great winding winter-lust around her.
>   Any man must feel
>   In him, the glacier's rammed carry
>   Of upheaval,
>   change,

A lockjaw concentration on his loins
Now glowing, inch-dreaming under the oval

Of the bell interruptedly cloven . . .

One wants to cry out the old *New Yorker* headline, "Stop that sentence!" But do these words even constitute real sentences? They feel more like casual accumulations of portentous phrases. In terms of sense, one can look very closely, but the vagueness never resolves into clarity. What are "outstaying / Life-longing intervals"? And as for "the glacier's rammed carry / Of upheaval, / change, / A lockjaw concentration on his loins / Now glowing, inch-dreaming," better not ask. As I said in my review, it takes a certain genius to write this badly.

Criticism should be a conversation about the experience of reading a literary work. It is not the paid patter of public relations; it should be an honest account of the critic's reactions. Our relation to a book—like most other things in life—is usually mixed. We like some aspects of a thing and not others. To articulate the slippery experience accurately is the challenge of criticism, even in the modest form of a book review. Literary culture depends on trust. The critic trusts the reader enough not to lie or condescend. He or she credits the reader with interest and intelligence. The reader, in turn, trusts the critic's veracity. Once that trust breaks down—as it has in today's poetry criticism—readers lose faith in the relationship because the reviewer treats them as inferiors to be hyped, patronized, or lectured. Readers cannot trust the praise of a critic who is not at times also willing to censure.

And so I tried to tell the truth. Because an honest review reflects the critic's emotions as well as ideas, I reflected my disappointment and annoyance along with my analysis. Rereading my piece now, I am struck most by the sadness with which I report Dickey's decline. Writing negative reviews is a necessary task, but it can present a moral danger to the critic who is tempted to gloat over an author's failure. Unless the author is a monster of ego—Norman Mailer or Gore Vidal, for example—the dismissal can be disproportionate to the occasion. It is too easy to indulge in cleverness and extravagant ridicule for its own sake. Such reviews may be fun to write (and delicious to read), but too many hatchet jobs can corrupt the critic, who soon becomes a public performer rather than a trustworthy confidant.

An interesting thing happened when I wrote about *Puella*. My assessment was initially part of a long group review, which I had allowed to exceed my assigned word count. Frederick Morgan, the co-editor of the *Hudson Review*, suggested that rather than shorten the discussions of each volume, I might just drop one book from the piece and publish that section elsewhere. That struck me as an attractive idea. Several editors had recently asked me to send them poetry reviews. I proposed that we drop the section on *Puella*. Morgan agreed, "The book isn't any good, and poor Dickey has already been knocked around in our pages." I then expanded my critique of *Puella* and sent it to the *Ontario Review* whose editors had repeatedly asked me for critical prose.

The piece came back immediately with the excuse that the journal had no space left in upcoming issues. I first sensed then what I now know; most small magazine editors do not want to run negative reviews, especially of influential writers. Most reviews are published to reward friends and allies. Or they praise "the usual suspects" to endorse the current consensus and to demonstrate that the journal knows which way the wind is blowing. If a negative piece occasionally appears—and some journals never run one—it attacks a representative figure from an ideologically opposed camp. In such cases, the editors prefer a general denunciation of an aesthetic and not a considered critique of an individual volume, especially not one that accepts a poet's premise while faulting the performance. In my youthful innocence I didn't yet know those unspoken rules.

I sent my review off to another editor. He was forthright enough to say that he didn't want to publish a negative piece. Finally, I sent it to Paul Lake, who had just helped start a tiny magazine called *Nebo* in Russellville, Arkansas. He took the piece, and it was printed in a journal so obscure I reasonably assumed—in those pre-Internet days—that no one beyond the environs of Russellville would ever see it.

Of course, I was mistaken. As I discovered several years later, the review had been not only seen but remembered. How did I find out? James Dickey told me—in the most vivid terms possible.

The occasion was the Library of Congress's 1987 Consultants' Reunion. This sumptuous literary gathering celebrated both the fiftieth anniversary of the Library's Consultantship in Poetry and the creation of the new Poet Laureate position. The Library had invited all sixteen living former consultants, a starry cast that included Gwendolyn Brooks, Anthony Hecht, Daniel Hoffman, Maxine Kumin, Howard Nemerov, Karl Shapiro, William Jay Smith, Stephen Spender, and William Stafford, as well as the first official laureate, Robert Penn Warren. And, of course, James Dickey. Each of the former consultants had been asked to invite a promising younger poet. I was lucky enough to be selected by Smith. Having published my first collection only the previous year (and still working full time at General Foods), I had no experience with literary high life and was eager to attend. I managed to get three days off work and headed to Washington.

The Consultants' Reunion could hardly have been better managed. Amid fancy dinners, lunches, and cocktail parties, each of the former consultants gave a reading, as did each of the younger poets. Senator Spark M. Matsunaga of Hawaii, the Congressional champion of the U.S. laureateship, had spent twenty-two years trying to establish the new public office. He beamed from the podium as he saluted the nation's first poet laureate. Of course, no piece of federal legislation is as simple as it seems in the press release. Officially, the Ninety-ninth Congress did not create the position of U.S. Poet Laureate; it enacted legislation that recognized the Library's existing Consultantship as "equivalent to that of Poet Laureate of the United States" and specified that the position henceforth be known as the "Poet Laureate Consultant in Poetry." Leave it to lawyers to honor poetry with so infelicitous a job title.

I had never experienced anything quite like the three-day affair. One could not even go to the bagel shop around the corner from the hotel without bumping into Lord and Lady Spender. (I ordered sesame. They chose plain.) I had arrived.

What fun would life be, however, without complications? In Washington, mine was quite simple. Among the fifty or so official speakers and guests were half a dozen authors, mostly old and influential, whose work I had given negative or mixed reviews. Common sense suggested I not go out of my way to meet them. This course of action was easy to manage, since all the events were very crowded. I did not reckon, however, on the tracking powers of the author of *Deliverance*.

For two days I avoided being introduced to Dickey. He was a big, beefy man with a loud voice—easy to spot and elude. On the last evening, however, there was a small cocktail party limited to the former consultants, their protégés, academic dignitaries, and library staff. Dickey was brought over to my group by a well-meaning librarian. There was no time to escape, and introductions were made.

Hearing my name, the poet paused, repeated it, and stared at me pensively. I thought it highly unlikely that he had read the review. I had never met anyone who had read *Nebo*. To be honest, I had never met anyone who had heard of it, except the editor.

"Day-na . . . Joy-a," he said again slowly in his thick Georgian accent.

Dickey was already drunk, but his flushed face, slurred speech, and lumbering movement suggested a decline beyond the effects of alcohol. The robust outdoorsman-poet of the tabloids had become a tottering wreck. His once solid frame now seemed both shrunken and bloated. His eyes were glassy. Worst of all, there was an alarmingly deep indentation on his upper forehead, as if he had sustained some serious head injury. For several moments he stood there. He said almost nothing and hardly attended to what the others said to him.

At the first convenient moment I slipped out of the group and joined another conversation across the room. Soon Dickey stumbled toward my new circle. He made no introductions, but stared at me, nodding slowly but decisively.

"Dana . . . Gioia . . . you write . . . reviews."

"Yes, I do."

He paused—as if he were about to leave, but once again he stood there silently. Someone made small talk. I went to the bar for a second drink. I then joined yet another small group. Dickey followed.

"Dana Gioia," he repeated emphatically.

"Yes?"

"You reviewed *my* book!"

"Yes, sir, I did."

"You didn't like it!"

"No, sir, I didn't."

I cannot do full justice to his reply, which reminded me of nothing so much as Molly Bloom's soliloquy from *Ulysses*, but I'll do my best to recreate a bit of it.

"Goddamn! You reviewers are all the same. You just don't understand. I am *not* Dick Wilbur! I gotta grow, goddammit, I am not Dick Wilbur! When you gonna understand that? You're all the same. All the same. I gotta grow, gotta try new things. Gotta. All you want is the same damn thing. You're all the same. Why don't you gimme room! Gotta grow, goddammit! I am not Dick Wilbur!"

He sputtered. He spat. He waved his fist. His drink splashed in his hand. The three or four party-goers beside me stood horror-struck. Soon others nearby had stopped talking and stared while Dickey roared on.

". . . You're all the same you wanna put me in some goddamn box I gotta grow gotta have room gotta who do you think I am I am not Dick Wilbur!"

After a few minutes, I realized that he was not planning to stop. He seemed too sad a figure to argue with, and too far gone that evening to approach in any rational way. And so I reached out, took his hand, and shook it warmly. "How nice to meet you, Mr. Dickey," I said. I held his hand and smiled. Then I walked away.

He stood there for a moment, caught in midsentence. His sudden silence made it obvious how quiet the crowded room had become during his booming monologue. No one moved or spoke. Then he nodded at his remaining interlocutors and lurched back toward the bar.

People in beautiful dark suits stared at me, wondering what obnoxious thing I had done to provoke this elder eminence. I found myself sweating and fidgeting under their cold, steady gazes. There was nothing to be done. I started up another conversation. It would not be the last unpleasant commotion I encountered in literary life. But no one ever brought such style and exuberance to the event. No wonder I still like those early poems.

Letters from the Bahamas

MEMOIR OF A POET I NEVER MET

Photograph © Stanley Toogood

I

I never met Ronald Perry, though I feel I knew him very well. Years ago when I was writing a "Poetry Chronicle" for the *Hudson Review*, I came across a collection unlike the other forty volumes piled on my desk. The book was Ronald Perry's *Denizens*, just published in the newly inaugurated and otherwise disappointing National Poetry Series. Never having heard of Perry, I was surprised to see four previous collections listed under the author's credits. How could I have missed his work until now? Later I was to learn that his impressive bibliography was somewhat misleading.

The poems in *Denizens* were technically brilliant but in a quiet, undramatic way—rather like a violinist playing through a difficult cadenza double pianissimo. Likewise, although one could occasionally see a touch of Auden or Stevens in his lines, the poems were highly original, often surprising the reader by taking unexpected turns. Having just suffered though several flat and featureless new volumes, I was also impressed by Perry's sophisticated sense of verse music. Here actually was poetry composed, as Pound demanded, "in the sequence of the musical phrase, not in sequence of a metronome." I did not know then that the author had once hoped to be a composer, but one could not miss his concern for the tone and timbre of words. Some poems even seemed to be written solely for musical and imagistic effects, a sort of *poésie pure* that hearkened back to the beginnings of modernism.

Denizens was also distinctive in another way. It was subtle and complex. Although contemporary poetry is widely held to be innovative and uncompromisingly difficult, most new verse—ask any honest reviewer— is simple and formulaic, sometimes even cozy. Perry's work, by contrast, made few accommodations to the reader. The sound was beguiling, but the sense was intricate and often elusive. His poems did not lay out every step for the reader but demanded active collaboration in making connections, especially in pursuing the possible associations of the metaphors and images. Here is "Nocturne":

One night, these dreams, as black
As horses, will surely
Overwhelm us—the terminal
Troops, parading superbly
To the sound of the bells
Splitting the sides
Of the churches, the lost
Silver speech
Of the trumpets, the last
Vestige of all that we have had
Stripped, crashing in cymbals
All around us—
What shall we say then
to those we have left
Disarmed, defenseless, behind us?

Perry also played with degrees of ambiguity in his work, purposely leaving out important details (usually the specific place or person addressed) to force the reader into keeping open a range of potential meanings. This deliberate ambiguity made *Denizens* a difficult book to read, especially for the first time. Many readers might give up on certain poems, feeling they cannot comprehend the full meaning. Ambiguity is a dangerous technique in poetry. When it works, it can create a mysterious and haunting atmosphere, a sense that the ultimate meaning lies just out of reach. When it fails, it results in pretense and obscurity. *Denizens* delivered its share of both outcomes, but its successes more than compensated for its failures.

Finally, there was an alluring impulse of sensual excitement in reading *Denizens*. What landscapes it described! What images evoked! One had to go back to Stevens to find another poet so fascinated with the gaudy and exotic. The book ranged from the desolate Pine Barrens of the Bahamas to jungle mountaintops in Laos with stops along the way in Mexico, Hungary, and Hell. Perry's imagination, however, habitually returned to florid tropical scenes, which, unlike Stevens, he knew first hand. Even his titles revealed his love for the bright and colorful—"The Guilt of the Gold Flower," "O banyan with beautiful leaves," "Tiger-Balm Gardens." His small bestiary contained a peacock, phoenix, hawk, and centaur, accompanied by only one ordinary goat.

All of these virtues, however, did not make

Denizens a perfect collection. It contained some uninspired poems, and others which, although touched by brilliance, were vitiated by ambiguity and even secrecy. I was also troubled by the lack of a unifying voice throughout the volume. *Denizens* seemed at times more like an anthology of different poets than a collection by a single author. But the book captivated me. Whatever faults Perry had as a writer were his own, not ones borrowed from his contemporaries. I wrote a review as part of a long survey of thirteen new books by authors including Joseph Brodsky, Ted Hughes, Kingsley Amis, Vicki Hearne, Ted Kooser, and two classical Chinese poets. My review wasn't a rave. It was a mixed and candid assessment in which I tried to communicate both the book's special fascination and frustrations.

Several months after my "Poetry Chronicle" appeared, I received a letter, forwarded from the *Hudson Review*. The blue envelope bore a return address in the Bahamas. I had no notion of what it could be, but on opening it, I saw Perry's signature. The note read:

> This is something I've not done before, almost certainly won't do again, and will undoubtedly continue to doubt the propriety of, even whilst I'm about it. But "Wot the Hell," as Mehitabel said to Archy on another occasion. I liked your "Poetry Chronicle" in the current *Hudson* a lot, including the review of *Denizens*, so why not tell you so? It seems to me

137

the most interesting, and perceptive, view of my
book I've yet seen, and it also makes me want rather
urgently to buy, and read several of the others. If, as
I think, that's the most important single objective of
any critic, you've succeeded, admirably.

How could I not be flattered? I wrote Perry a short
note thanking him for his letter.

Nine months later another letter from Perry arrived. This one was longer, full of interesting news
and opinions. Toward the end Perry asked if I would
be willing to read the manuscript of a new book he
was preparing. He was isolated in the Bahamas, he
explained, and had to rely almost entirely on the advice of two old friends from his Miami days, Donald Justice and Laurence Donovan. Would I be willing to give an outside opinion? I was surprised by the
request. "Wot the Hell," I said to myself. I told him to
send me the manuscript.

From this point on, Perry wrote me with increas-
ing regularity. Soon I was receiving letters or packets
two or three times a week. It seemed I couldn't open
my mailbox without finding a thick blue envelope
covered in extravagant Bahamian stamps and stuffed
with poems. There was no way I could keep up with
this stream of correspondence, but he repeatedly
urged me not to try. I wrote back as often as I could.
I sensed that he was content just to have an apprecia-
tive reader. Under usual circumstances I might have
become annoyed at so much mail from one person,

but I was charmed by Perry's witty and intelligent letters, which sometimes ran for six or seven pages, typed single spaced. And the poems! I was amazed by both their quantity and quality. He was onto something new and was pursuing it wholeheartedly. Of course, the work he sent was uneven, but here and there were splendid individual poems as good and sometimes even better than anything in *Denizens*.

In early July, Perry wrote that he was coming to New York on a holiday. Could we meet? I replied to set a date, and we made plans for an evening together. Perry provided a phone number in Brooklyn where he would be staying. Meanwhile I had picked up some free back issues of the *Hudson Review*, which contained Perry's uncollected prose. I thought he would enjoy having the extra copies.

A few days before our planned meeting, I received a packet in the mail. It included a note confirming our meeting along with a copy of Donald Justice's first collection, *The Old Bachelor and Other Poems* (1951). This small pamphlet published by Preston Dettman's Pandanus Press in Miami was so rare that it was not even listed in Justice's early bibliographies. Why would Perry give me so valuable a book, I wondered, especially his only copy of one by so special a friend? I meant to ask him about it when we met.

On the morning of July 14, I phoned his Brooklyn number to ask what time we should meet for dinner. A priest answered the phone. He told me Perry had died suddenly the night before.

II

Ronald Lee Perry was born in 1932 in Miami, Florida, then a smaller, more Southern town than today's teeming Latin metropolis. Most of his childhood, however, was spent further south in Rock Harbor, a small settlement on Key Largo where his parents operated a commercial fishing lodge. He studied at the University of Miami where in his sophomore year he met Donald Justice who was a young instructor there. The two became lifelong friends. In 1954 Perry left the university having completed an MA in English Literature and History. He spent two years in the U.S. Army as a cryptographer—an experience one suspects had some influence on his poetry. In 1956 Perry was discharged from the military to accept a writing fellowship at the University of Iowa. He left the elite program after only six weeks, having begun just one course in Anglo-Saxon. He claimed that returning to graduate school made him realize that he did not want to teach for a living. Privately he also confessed that he disliked the arrogance of the students in the program. He felt his own writing could be done better outside the academy.

Returning to Miami, Perry found work as an airline reservation agent. About this time he published his first collection, *The Fire Nursery and Other Poems* (1956), a letterpress pamphlet of only four poems printed in Miami by Preston Dettman. Perry then began a period of travel that eventually brought him to Vientiane, Laos where he worked as a secretary for an engineering firm in the uneasy years between the French withdrawal and the American occupation. Laos made a profound impression on Perry's imagination inspiring his longest prose work, a series of traditional Laotian tales, which he freely adapted into English. It also inspired what is perhaps his finest poem, the haunting sequence, "After the Lao."

In 1959 Perry's first full-length collection, *The Rock Harbor*, appeared from the indefatigable independent publisher Alan Swallow in Denver. A few months later another pamphlet appeared, *The Pipe Smokers: An Eclogue for an Unspecified Occasion* (1960), once again printed by Dettman in a limited edition. About this time Perry moved to Nassau, Bahamas. For the next eleven years he worked for Outboard Marine International, first as a bookkeeper, and then, having been promoted, he claimed, against his will, as Director of Advertising and Public Relations. He published *Voyages from Troy* (1962), a poorly produced booklet from "Mariner Press" in Miami. The self-published pamphlet contains a rambling mythological sequence illustrated by Laurence Donovan. Like his earlier collections, *Voyages from Troy* made little impression beyond a coterie of Miami-based friends. Isolated and unsuccessful, Perry lost interest in writing. A few more poems and Laotian tales appeared in *Poetry* and the *Hudson Review*. By the end of the decade Perry had stopped writing.

When *Denizens* appeared in 1980, Perry was a forgotten poet. It had been eighteen years since his last volume and twenty-one since his only full collection. His books were all out of print. His work had never received critical attention or been reprinted in anthologies. Living outside the academy, Perry had no professional network of colleagues or students. His reputation survived mostly among his friends.

One friend proved decisive. Random House published Perry's new collection, *Denizens*, through the intervention of Donald Justice who had been asked to choose one of the five initial volumes of the National Poetry series. At first, Justice and Perry planned a retrospective volume, but inspired by the project, Perry began writing again, and the final *Denizens* contained mostly new work.

The publication of *Denizens* brought Perry's literary career back to life. It put him in touch with other poets and reminded editors of his existence. Most important, it filled him with the confidence to continue writing. Now retired from his business career, Perry threw all his energy into poetry. Within a year of *Denizens'* publication he had written enough poems for a new collection. The new work differed in style from his earlier poems. It was more expansive and accessible, its structure less musical and more narrative. Whereas the work in *Denizens* lacked a cohesive voice, these new pieces shared a recognizable personal perspective.

As he turned fifty in January in 1982, Perry was excitedly planning his literary future. *Denizens* had received excellent reviews. His new manuscript, *In the*

Smoke, was with his editor Gary Fisketjon at Random House. Perry was nervously planning the first public reading of his career—at his alma mater, University of Miami. He had been invited to speak at their poetry festival with Richard Wilbur, Dave Smith, and William Empson. Anxious about his debut, Perry scripted his entire reading, preparing and compulsively revising a twenty-nine-page typescript of poems and commentary. Much to his surprise, he enjoyed the event and was eagerly planning another reading on National Public Radio.

Perry now entered the most productive period of his literary life sometimes sketching out four or five new poems a week while frenetically reworking half a dozen others. "I feel like a factory again," he wrote in a letter. He had prepared almost enough work for two volumes—a drastically revised version of *In the Smoke* and a dark, premonitory collection of Bahamian poems—when he died suddenly in Nassau on July 13, 1982. He had been writing up to the day of his death. An unfinished poem was found in his typewriter.

III

Death settles most things. It also sets new events in motion.

On the morning of July 14, I was in my office at General Foods in White Plains, New York, expecting to meet Perry that evening in Manhattan. I phoned the Brooklyn number he had given me. Father Walter Mitchell answered the phone. He told me that Perry had never arrived. Then after a pause, he added, "Ronald killed himself last night in Nassau." He offered no details. He was distraught. We were two strangers. Neither of us knew what to say. I put the phone down in a state of shock. I stumbled through the rest of my day. It wasn't only sadness. It was confusion. Nothing in Perry's lively letters had suggested suicide.

Late in the afternoon I received a second phone call, this one from the Bahamas. It was a man named John Carson. As we spoke, I realized he was Perry's partner, though back then no one used that neutered term. Carson told me that Ronald had not killed himself. He had suffered a heart attack while starting his car. It had initially seemed like suicide, he admitted, but the police had declared it death by natural causes.

Carson then asked if I could help notify Ronald's friends about his death. I replied that I had never met Ronald, and we had only a handful of common friends. Carson, however, was not only desperate; he was also outside the U.S. And international calls were difficult and expensive. I agreed to help.

That evening I phoned our few mutual acquaintances—Donald Justice, Emily Grosholz, Frederick Morgan, and Harry Duncan. I gave Justice a complete account of both phone calls with their differing versions of Perry's death. He had known Perry for thirty years. He deserved all the facts as I knew them. To the others, I said only that Perry had suffered a heart attack. Justice promised to call the members of their old Miami group.

Telling a person that a common friend has died is never a short phone call. One repeats the bad news several times in slightly different words. It takes a few minutes for reality to settle in. Then both parties reflect on the grim event, which touches uncomfortably on their own mortality. Questions are asked and speculations ventured. Everyone feels the obligation to share memories, usually happy ones. Soon it is no longer a conversation. It becomes a ritual that both parties feel the need to enact, though often neither speaker understands the rules.

When I hung up the phone for the last time, my voice was hoarse. I went to bed exhausted but too distressed to sleep. I had done what I promised. The funeral would be far away in Nassau. My brief relationship with Perry was at an end.

The next day I got more phone calls. I was not surprised to hear again from Carson and Mitchell. What I had not expected were the calls from strangers. Perry's Miami friends started phoning. The callers asked if I had more information than Justice had provided. Then they began to speculate on the situation. I told them I knew nothing more, so they told me what had really happened. Half of them claimed it was suicide. One person even stated that Perry had hanged himself. Others said it was a heart attack or a stroke. He had felt ill and got in his car to drive to the hospital but died before he got out of the garage.

They also shared their memories of Perry. They spoke longingly of Coconut Grove in the 1950s, Miami's lost bohemia, which fostered a small community of artists, musicians, and writers. The city had been smaller, calmer, less expensive. The stories they told about Perry were amiable and generic—nights of drinking, smoky jazz clubs, midnight swims at the beach, early dreams of artistic fame, and love affairs. They were elegies to youth in a vanished paradise of palm trees and moonlit beaches. There were also a few dubious disclosures. One caller asserted that Perry had spent his years in Laos involved in espionage. I thought he worked for Outboard Marine, I replied. "Just a cover," the person declared.

Justice wrote to ask if I could suggest a few lines from Perry's poetry that could go on a memorial notice. Of course, he had already found the perfect passage. Opening *Denizens* at random, he had employed a process "akin to divination" to land on a few lines from "Voices." It was impossible to improve on his suggestion:

But if we return in the small hours
Between midnight and morning
Surely someone will hear us?

After a few days the calls stopped, though I felt no better informed about Perry's final moments. Exactly a month after the death, Justice wrote to say that he had spoken to Carson who had read him the autopsy report:

The story is that Ronald did *not* commit suicide, though the circumstances were ambiguous enough on the surface to suggest that he had done so . . . it can now be assumed that Ronald, alone in the house in Nassau late at night, suffering one of the terrible headaches he'd been having and not being able to reach his doctor by phone, got in his car to drive to the doctor or the hospital, and at that time was overwhelmed by a sort of stroke . . . I gather that the motor had continued to run, thus leading to the suspicion of self-murder, though there was no note.

Justice declared he had no reason to question the story. Nor did I, though rumors of suicide persisted. There had been nothing suicidal in Perry's letters or poems. He had been excited by his creative rebirth and had looked forward to his New York visit. Justice said that we needed to get Perry's new poems printed. I informed Justice that I had begun a short memoir about my epistolary friendship with Perry. So began another primal ritual, creating something to commemorate the dead. Keeping the memory of the departed alive is an expression of love or esteem; it is also a means of deflecting our own eventual oblivion.

By now I had recognized how odd my situation was. I, who had never met Ronald Perry, had become the focal point for memorializing him. I placed a number of poems in small magazines. Everyone was eager to publish them. There remained the larger problem, however, of bringing out Perry's final book.

The problem wasn't merely finding a publisher for the collection, though this was an issue. Gary Fisketjon at Random House declined to return calls or letters about Perry's manuscript. New York's celebrity editor had little use for a book by a nearly unknown poet from another country. Nothing sells worse than poetry, except the work of a dead poet.

A more complicated problem was figuring out what exactly constituted Perry's final volume, which existed in multiple versions in the hands of different correspondents. Even the title was uncertain. Perry referred to it interchangeably as *Smoke* and *In the Smoke*. The different manuscripts had different tables of content. I myself had three or four versions, none of them dated. Even the poems existed in different versions. That confusion only described what we had actually seen. None of us had examined Perry's own manuscripts back in Nassau. We began to collate our versions. There were problems on nearly every page.

Meanwhile I finished a short memoir based on Perry's letters, books, and information from his friends. I sent it and a memorial poem to *Cumberland Poetry Review*, which I had convinced to run an extensive feature on Perry. I also sent copies of the typescript to Justice and Duncan.

I had come to know Duncan over the previous few years because the two of us were working on the first collection of stories by Weldon Kees. To me, Duncan was a living legend, the patriarch of modern American fine press printing. His Cummington Press, which he founded in 1941 with artist Wrightman Williams, had published an astonishing list of books in striking hand printed editions. Among many other titles, Cummington had issued *Notes Toward a Supreme Fiction* by Wallace Stevens, *Land of Unlikeness* by Robert Lowell, *The Hovering Fly* by Allen Tate, *The Wedge* by William Carlos Williams, and *Blackberry Winter* by Robert Penn Warren.

To my astonishment, Duncan replied by return post that he wanted to print the memoir and the poem at Abattoir Editions, his new imprint at the University of Nebraska, Omaha. He had known Perry thirty years earlier. Reading the pieces, Duncan had suddenly conceived a page design he wanted to realize. "I've always been interested in mixtures of poetry and prose," he wrote citing Dante's *La Vita Nuova* and Yeats's *A Vision*. "And now you provide a poem and prose that clearly belong together, and summon the typographer to work that's more than mere decoration." I assumed that the proposed book would be a slow and uncertain project. Fine presses move at a measured pace. Hand-set typography and letterpress printing takes time. Projects are often delayed or cancelled. Duncan and I had already been working for three years on the Kees collection.

I guessed wrong. Two weeks after reading the memoir—a period which included both Christmas and New Year's Day—Duncan sent me the first proof of *Letter to the Bahamas*, which he had laid out on huge folio pages. He had designed the work to resemble a medieval book in which a poetic text was enclosed by prose commentary. He put each stanza of my poem on its own page where it was surrounded on all four sides by the prose memoir. Twelve weeks later the large and elegant book was published. In the meantime two other notable fine press printers, Kim Merker of Windover Press and Michael Peich of Aralia Press, had announced their interest in publishing Perry's collection, though the length of the book intimidated them. Duncan also said he would like to bring the volume out. A sample manuscript was circulated while Emily and I tried to determine Perry's final intentions.

By then John Carson had gone silent. He had been ordained an Anglican deacon a few weeks after Perry's death. Perhaps he needed to put the sad affair behind him. We now had no access to Perry's own manuscripts. It was unclear who controlled the estate, unclear even if there was an estate. Had his papers been saved when Perry's house was cleaned out? What had happened to the final poem left in his typewriter? Had it even existed? From New York it was impossible to ascertain the situation in Nassau. We were all busy with our own lives. I was working full time at General Foods and trying to finish my first book in the evenings. Random House was incommunicado. None of the fine presses made a firm offer. The project was postponed. We waited hopefully, but we waited in vain.

Several of Perry's friends sent me things—a pamphlet, old magazines, poems, and even letters. This, too, I realized, was a ritual. They sought to honor his memory, perhaps even to exorcise whatever guilt they felt about the situation. They wanted certain things saved and didn't know where else to send them. Perhaps my status as a stranger made me the inevitable recipient—I broadened the circle of memory.

The most significant gift was a file of twenty-five years of letters from Perry to Maggie Donovan DuPriest. She was the former wife of Laurence Donovan, the artist and poet who had collaborated with Perry in his Coconut Grove years. I didn't understand why Maggie DuPriest had sent me the extensive file of Perry's personal correspondence—dozens of long letters, single-spaced, some running for several pages. Once I read them I understood. Perry had poured out his heart to her. He described his life, his work, and the end of his tortured relationship with "Jimmy," a painter. The intimate and often lyrical letters also revealed a growing love affair with DuPriest (who was then still married to Donovan). They also disclosed not one but two overlapping romantic triangles. Perry wrote candidly about his sexuality, which he considered fixed and permanent, but had left him lonely and unhappy. He discussed the possibilities of marriage with Maggie if she divorced. There could be no sexual union, he declared, but there would be love. The letters boil with emotion—longing, regret, hope, anxiety, and desire. "What are we going to do?" he writes. *"We must decide and soon."*

The marriage was not to be, and soon each party ended up with a partner more appropriate to his or her libido. They both understood that their affectionate love, however genuine, was not enough to sustain a lifelong union. Their friendship continued without a ripple. Perry's letters also contained a fascinating account of interviewing with the State Department, which had discovered in his security clearance that he was homosexual. He described their insulting, bureaucratic way of noting but ignoring the information. From this account, it seems unlikely that he had become a spy.

Perry had asked DuPriest to burn the letters she gave me. He was not the first lover to have such a request ignored. She not only kept them but arranged them chronologically in metal-tabbed legal file folders. The letters provided a vivid first-person account of Perry's personal and artistic life. They also joined her and Perry permanently in a web of words. The letters had been entrusted to me for safekeeping. They were the sort of thing a friend or family member might destroy after her death. She surely hoped that others would read them after the deaths of the people involved. The correspondence became part of a growing archive about Perry's life and career I had passively accumulated.

I was twenty-nine when I published my review of *Denizens*. I knew a great deal about literature but almost nothing about literary life. I worked in an office. I wrote in the evening. I read late into the night. No one at the company knew I was a writer. I led a queer sort of literary life, solitary and furtive. What I knew about the lives of poets came from books. Yet I was trying, mostly by intuition, to discern my own path into the art.

Poetry obsessed me, but it existed somewhere else—in the past, in classrooms, behind the doors of editorial offices—certainly nowhere in my vicinity. Nothing in my exacting outer life—what everyone called "the real world"—touched the passions that secretly constituted my real life. I had constructed a mental wall to protect my imagination from the pressures and preoccupations of my career. I felt that if I could keep my two lives separate, I could manage the stress of my ten-hour days and nightly labor.

I often thought about Wallace Stevens, who had spent thirty-nine years at Hartford Accident and Indemnity. I admired his stubborn determination to keep the world at a distance. He worked in an office, wrote in the evenings, and did almost nothing else. I catalogued the renunciations he found necessary to preserve his creative clarity. I made my own sacrifices and abstentions. For five years I had even stopped sending out poems. I was dissatisfied with what I had published. I kept writing in private. Whatever it was I sought I had to find myself. I gave over my nights and weekends, month after month, to the slow discovery and refinement of my own voice. I survived by living in the future tense. Stevens, whose career had been marked by long silences, was the perfect model. As an artist, he had required nothing except a little time and space in which to write. He had created masterpieces. His example was magnificent, compelling, and inhuman.

This was my life when Ronald Perry first wrote me—disciplined, intellectual, and excessively introspective. It had to change. There was much to learn from Stevens, but I wanted more engagement with life, though I wasn't quite sure how. Then, unexpectedly, change came. I, who had so carefully avoided human drama, found myself in the midst of one.

My friendship with Perry had a fantastic quality—an invisible poet writing from a tropical island, a quick camaraderie marked by mutual generosity. How strange it would seem to a young writer today— a friendship between strangers conceived and sustained solely by letters in the post. It lasted a single year. Then came his sudden death on the eve of our first meeting. I never spoke to Perry. I never even saw a photograph until after his death. The story seems outlandish in the telling.

I didn't understand the strangeness of literary life until the aftermath of Perry's death. It wasn't a rational and orderly existence; it was impulsive, mysterious, and uncertain. I knew its necessary solitude and dedication, but I had not appreciated the endurance it required in the face of endless insecurity, thwarted ambition, and frequent failure—hardships hardly offset by occasional success and recognition. It was a fragile existence made tolerable, sometimes even redeemed, by the intoxication of creation and intensity of literary friendship. When Perry died, he left me his friends, most notably Donald Justice. He and I had known each other for several years. It had been a respectful and intellectual connection, always touched by a certain caution. Suddenly our shared sorrow created an emotional bond. We discovered a relaxed and intimate friendship that lasted until Justice's death twenty years later.

Few people remember Ronald Perry or his work. His original circle of friends is mostly gone. What remains of their dreams, feuds, and love affairs sits undisturbed in boxes in the University of Miami library. Perry's work was little read in his lifetime, except for the brief flurry of attention for *Denizens*. All of it is out of print, much of it never published. Perry made only one public appearance. He never gave an interview. When I search the Internet, I find only my old memoir or short biographical entries based on it, often verbatim. Had he lived another ten or twenty years, he might have made a more enduring impression. Instead, dead at fifty, he vanished.

Oblivion is the fate of most poets. Yet writing down these memories of Ronald Perry, I know that my account will not be the last that readers encounter. Someone will explore his legacy—another impulsive and curious stranger. Not soon perhaps, but eventually. Camerado, I give you my hand. Let's remember the friends we loved and those we never met. Oblivion can do its work elsewhere. Remembrance is our métier. After all, our Muse is the daughter of Memory.

Postscript

BEING OUTTED

When I entered corporate life, I resolved to keep my writing secret. There was no advantage in being known as the company poet. For nearly a decade I succeeded in keeping my double life hidden from my co-workers. Whenever something of mine appeared in the *New Yorker*, I would discreetly buy all five copies in the company shop, mail one to my parents, and slip the others into the bottom of the finance department's bulging recycling bin.

There was little chance of my colleagues seeing the other journals in which I published, although once a brainy summer intern asked if I had written an article he had seen in the *Hudson Review*. "My brother recently wrote something for them," I replied not untruthfully and quickly changed the subject.

In 1984, however, *Esquire* permanently blew my cover when I was featured in the first "Esquire Register of Men and Women Under Forty Who Are Changing America." Someone brought a copy of the issue into the office and passed it around. Had it been merely a literary honor, no one would have noticed, but here was the name of a General Foods execu-tive on a list with really important people like Julius "Doctor J." Erving, Whoopi Goldberg, Dale Murphy, and Steven Spielberg.

At that time I worked for the most macho boss in the company, an Annapolis graduate, All-American athlete, and former commanding officer of combat longshoremen (the lucky guys who unload military supplies under enemy fire). He was a brilliant, hot-tempered, fellow who didn't waste words. For exam-ple, he addressed his close associates only by their initials. I was summoned by a secretary to his office where he sat smoking a cigar butt. He motioned me to come closer.

"D.G., someone told me you wrote poetry."

"Yeah, Greg," I replied. "I do."

He took the greasy stub out of his mouth, ground it into the ashtray, and whispered, not unkindly, only one word, "Shit."

Appendix

A CONVERSATION WITH JOHN CHEEVER

Here is the transcript of the conversation with John Cheever from January 23, 1976. In its original published form, this expansive interview was reduced to six pages. Many interesting comments and observations were lost. The transcript is complete except for a few remarks that Cheever wished to remain off record.

DANA GIOIA: Mr. Cheever, do you consider that there is a consistently good market for quality fiction in America?

JOHN CHEEVER: No, alas, I don't, and it's an enormous dilemma for people of your generation. The number of magazines has, in the space of perhaps twenty years, gone from something like fourteen to perhaps one-and-a-half or two. It makes publication very difficult. For your generation recognition of any sort is difficult to achieve. One can only hope the situation will improve.

MILLICENT DILLON: I want to ask you about "The Swimmer." I wondered if you could say something about the origin of that story?

CHEEVER: Oh, yes, I can. I'm very fond of the story. I suppose the origin is simply the pleasure I took sitting at the edge of a swimming pool on a summer day on which everyone had drunk too much. Also, the story is more or less factual in that occasionally someone will come to the country to interview me and say, "Well, how did you think of the story?" And I say, "All right, well, get your trunks on and I'll show you"—and I'll take him through seven pools (which usually exhausts him). And he gets on the train, or drives home again. It was to have been a short story. I think there are thirteen pools in the story now. In the original version, there were something like forty-five. The notes for the story (which I burned) ran something like a hundred and fifty pages. I think the finished manuscript was something like fifteen. Any questions about the story seem to me to imply that the story has failed—it should be taken at its face value. The fact that the constellations change, that the foliage changes, that all time is completely dislocated or altered in the story, ought to be taken at face value. However, as a parody of what can be done academically with the story, you can begin with the level that this is simply a reference to Ovid. And this is Narcissus, of course, and it is his face that he is pursuing, and this is the pursuit of death. It can—from the Communist point of view (and it's a very popular story in Russia)—be an example of the artificiality of a personality based entirely on consumer consumption. You can cut down through about seven layers of the story, if you feel like it. I think it's an idle occupation and, if it can't be taken at its surface value, that is, if it doesn't have a response in the reader, then of course it's failed.

DILLON: I am curious about how you arrived at the tone of the story, which seemed so precisely perfect all the way along—whether that had taken a long time or whether you had arrived at it fairly quickly?

CHEEVER: The story took rather a long time. Most of the stories I like, however long they may be, forty or fifty pages, are usually written in three days. This took, I believe, two months. I was enormously happy with it. I don't think I've ever worked so long on a short story. I knew what I wanted, and . . . it is a sleight of hand.

MICHAEL STILLMAN: I was interested in how you feel about the use of fiction in making films. It seems to me that they're two very different kinds of art.

CHEEVER: I think they're vastly different. There's a clash between the two techniques. It seems to me that almost any competent novelist could write a fairly brilliant screenplay, but one is not writing a screenplay, of course, one is writing a novel. Saul Bellow's novels don't film; John Updike's novels don't film (to mention two colleagues I greatly esteem)—and I think my work doesn't film. Simply because if I come on a theme that could be handled more competently by a camera, I avoid it.

GIOIA: Do you think, then, that people in the first rank of American fiction right now have not been greatly influenced by the cinema or television?

CHEEVER: I think they've been influenced by it to the point that they're sophisticated. They know that very complex introspective sort of perception that one hopes to capture in a novel and the equally complex and introspective cadence that one has with a camera. Scenes are played out obviously for the camera eye rather than for the intellectual response of the novelist. I was in the hospital—as an example of something for a camera rather than for prose—and I had had a very bad heart attack, and had finally been unplugged, and the doctors and nurses said, "Christ, that was a close call!" (something like that), and they had taken everything out of me, and I was lying in bed in a hospital room that was extraordinarily bleak, as they are, except for the window curtains, which had been printed with poppies and foxglove and had obviously been chosen to cheer a man who was either dying or had just escaped death—this is a camera detail, rather than a prose detail. I don't think a respectable novelist would bother to describe the curtains, or he would see them but would cast the detail off. There was a knock on the door, and I opened it, and there was a young priest holding the paraphernalia for Holy Eucharist. I didn't think that I could say, "No, thank you," or "No, thanks." I didn't know what to say, so I backed into the room. He came in, and I said, "Shall I kneel?" And he said, "Yes, please." And I knelt on the cold linoleum in my pajamas, and he gave me Holy Communion. And at the end of the blessing, I said, "Thank you, Father," and he left. And I don't know where he came from or who he was. I've never seen him again. I never bothered to question him. But this would be much better with the camera than in prose, be much stronger. If you simply begin with the knock, the open door, go through the Mass, say nothing but the Mass—and the priest goes out. You could do it, of course, in fiction, but it's simply an example of what one recognizes as being better on film.

DILLON: So then, are you implying that television or film operates in a way to set up situations that the novelist will avoid? That it's narrowed the field?

CHEEVER: Rather it's broadened it. "Sophistication" is the word I would use. It has made the novelist aware of the fact that he has, more or less, this brother in the race who can handle certain scenes better than he. I still think that the retina used in reading prose is much more tenacious, much more lasting, than that which is taken off a screen, that a good prose paragraph, page, chapter, or book, lasts much longer than a splendid film.

STILLMAN: How do you feel about the role of the speaking voice in fiction?

CHEEVER: Well, it seems to me that having virtually a perfect ear is as rudimentary to a novelist as his kidney, for example. That you have to be able to catch accents, to overhear what is being said four tables away. This is simply literary kindergarten as far as I'm concerned. Then what you'd have to do, of course, is to exert a good deal of taste in what you use.

STILLMAN: How about the voice of the narrator?

CHEEVER: The omniscient narrator cutting in and out, of course, is something that was used widely in the eighteenth century, and we still employ it. The novelist is perfectly free to bring in any voice he wants. He actually enjoys more freedom, I suppose, than a filmmaker.

STILLMAN: Do your narrators change voice from story to story? Or would you say they're spoken pretty much in John Cheever's voice with John Cheever's tone?

CHEEVER: Well, I would hope they're not spoken in John Cheever's voice and in John Cheever's tone. Of course, they are. That's a battle I've lost.

DILLON: You have said fiction is not crypto-autobiography.

CHEEVER: What I usually say is, fiction is not crypto-autobiography: its splendor is that it is not autobiographical. Nor is it biographical. It is a very rich complex of autobiography and biography, of information—factual information, spiritual information, apprehension. It is the bringing together of disparate elements into something that corresponds to an aesthetic, a moral, a sense of fitness. I feel very strongly about the splendors of the imagination: how they have suffered in the post-Freudian generation is an endless source of anxiety.

GIOIA: Do you feel that there's a lot to be offered teaching creative writing? Is it a situation you feel comfortable in? And do you think that the students profit from it?

CHEEVER: Yes I do. Nobody likes the phrase "creative writing," of course. I try to call the classes, if I'm allowed, "Advanced Composition." It is, in my case, no more than a conversation between an old writer and a young writer. And the old writer has a great deal to learn and, in many cases, so has the young writer. It seems to me mutually a very good arrangement.

GIOIA: Do you give assignments?

CHEEVER: I give what is known as a drill. My favorite drills are: give me three pages on your imagined introspection of a jogger, write me a love letter written in a burning building, give me eight disparate incidents that are superficially alien and profoundly allied. I can't remember the other drills (I had about twenty). Flaubert used to drill de Maupassant, used to send him down to the Rouen railroad station where there were about twenty cab drivers and to tell him to describe each face in a sentence. Then Flaubert would go down and check and see how de Maupassant made out.

GIOIA: Do you think that much of the best fiction being written today is in short stories?

CHEEVER: No, it seems to me to be spread over short stories, novels, poetry, and plays. The forms are not competitive. It isn't the Short Story and the Novel in the Superbowl. They assist one another, they throw light on one another. They should.

STILLMAN: Occasionally, the concept of innovative fiction comes up. What would you say about innovative fiction?

CHEEVER: Well, fiction, of course, is innovative. My definition of fiction would be that it is heretical—fiction is one of our most valuable heresies. It is constantly questioning, and profoundly questioning, any paradigm. The fact that the novel is declared dead three times a year is its very nature, because it's a form of resurrection. It's a very powerful and chancy way of life. And we call novels (only in the English-speaking world) something meaning "newness" (this is the new way of looking at things)—in France and Italy, of course, they're still called romances (something we've never stooped to, or never been stuck with)—so that it's always a newness. The excitement of writing is that you are saying, in language that has never been used before, or in arrangements of language that have never been used before, something you don't know to have been recorded before. So it is always basically innovative. It is an exploratory and heretical pursuit. We then have experimentation, which is something of a spinoff from innovation: experimentation in what license one can take in using words in a nonverbal or inchoate sense. This seems to me generally unsuccessful. But fiction is innovative in its constant change of cadence. It lives on discovery.

GIOIA: What is your response to the school of American writers that one associates with John Barth and Donald Barthelme, influenced by Borges, who are innovative in that they use fiction to discuss almost abstract artistic questions?

CHEEVER: Oh, let's see if I can remember a quotation. I wrote a short story for a retiring editor of the *New Yorker*. [*Editor's note:* "The Folding-Chair Set," *New Yorker*, 13 October 1975.] There were a number of barbs in it. There was a paragraph, I'll try to remember it. "They were the sort of people that went around the world once or twice a year reading Borges and Barthelme in Statlers and Hiltons while the monsoon rains lashed the nearby temples they had come to see, but if you questioned their taste in reading, if"— there are too many "ifs" here—"if the world around you looks like Delacroix's *Death of Sardanopolis*, the charms of an empty canvas will seem irresistible." Right? Does that answer your question? That may be a little recondite. Do you understand what I mean?

DILLON: Among the younger people that you're dealing with, do you notice some kind of resistance to that kind of inchoate fiction?

CHEEVER: Yes, I think I do. Of course, I must speak within the confinements of my age. The only thing I think lamentable in these enthusiasms is the element of vogue, how people will seize on a book, not because it is particularly sympathetic, but because it is fashionable—and in the last, what, eight years, one has seen Hermann Hesse, for example, who was read by everyone not particularly because he was comprehended, but because it was rather like wearing skirts or trousers of a certain style. He was followed by Vonnegut, whom I think a very good man, but who again was a vogue writer, then Barth, Barthelme, Coover, and Gass—marvelous law firm!—all of whom I think extremely interesting. And John Gardner belongs in there. And, as a matter of fact, Doctorow. Very interesting, and very important people. I much prefer Coover.

GIOIA: Your own writing uses an almost traditional fictional viewpoint—an interest in social textures of class, of a person's position vis-à-vis society. Do you think that that's less of an interest among young short story writers?

CHEEVER: It seems to me that what one is dealing with is, and I still insist on this, that fiction is our most intimate and acute means of communication, at a profound level, about our deepest apprehensions and intuitions on the meaning of life and death. And that is what binds us together, young and old.

GIOIA: I noticed you made fun of a mythic reading of "The Swimmer," which would be a very natural reading for a lot of contemporary writers to give their works. Is that simply your comment on the texture of your work?

CHEEVER: Well, actually, when I commented on "The Swimmer," I was simply hinting lightly at the fact that it's much easier to teach fiction, not at the level of its success, but at the level of veterinary medicine, symbolism, or vivisection. It's much easier for teacher and easier for the student who has no particular interest in literature to dissect a story than to be moved by it.

DILLON: Have there been other people, a community of writers who have been supportive to you in any way, or individual writers who've been helpful to you?

CHEEVER: Yes, immensely. When I was seventeen or eighteen, I guess, I had the good fortune to meet Dos Passos, Edmund Wilson—Jim Agee was a contemporary I knew very well—Sherwood Anderson. It was Estlin Cummings who, through a similarity in background, made it quite clear to me that one could be a writer and also remain highly intelligent, totally independent, and be married to one of the most beautiful women in the world. Cummings was a complete revelation and an enormous help, and I loved him dearly.

GIOIA: You mentioned before that Bellow's *Humboldt's Gift* had been received with bewildering reviews. Are you happy with the state of reviewing in American magazines and newspapers?

CHEEVER: Well, I haven't known anything different, so I wouldn't have anything to compare—you know, anything that would strike me as being a happier time. In Europe, there are many more critics, actually, than we have here in the United States. In Russia, literature still is of much more importance to the lives of the people than it is in the United States. German, French, and Italian reviews are inclined to criticism—and, by criticism, I mean perhaps the illumination, or a report on the pleasure that the reader has taken in the work. In America, much more than in Europe, we have literary journalism and then literary criticism. And the journalist's responsibility is to report the price of the book, the number of the pages, the nature of the book. As a newspaper reporter, in many cases, he's not competent to judge the book; and in many cases, he will, in spite of his incompetence, go ahead. But my feeling is that books have a vitality that is invincible and, quite independently of either stupid or intelligent reviews, they will go to the millions (I think no less than millions) of people in the world who enjoy books, who enjoy fiction, who enjoy serious and innovative fiction.

GIOIA: Do you see yourself writing to any particular audience?

CHEEVER: No, I don't think that anyone can see an audience anymore. I think that came rather to a marked conclusion—or at least an obvious illustration is Virginia Woolf who, in her best books was addressing a very well-defined population. And, since that time, it seems to me, no writer has really known to whom he was speaking. To the people who are literate, obviously, but it would be very hard to describe them.

GIOIA: Does that affect your writing?

CHEEVER: I think not. If it has any effect at all, I suppose it would be an enlargement. The fact that one doesn't know to whom one is speaking, but that they are there, is perhaps a more satisfactory experience than knowing precisely, as Mrs. Woolf did, where they lived, what they ate, and when they went to bed.

STILLMAN: Are there particular kinds of innovation in the works of your contemporaries that you admire and have learned from?

CHEEVER: Saul Bellow's work is endlessly innovative—no novel is like the other, no story is like the other, no sentence is like the other in Saul's work. Saul will chop sentence, sentence, sentence for a paragraph, then cut it off with two pieces of slang from the twenties. John Updike is also innovative. I don't know why I should pick these two men. Flannery O'Connor was highly innovative. Faulkner was innovative. Hemingway was enormously innovative.

STILLMAN: What kinds of innovation impress you the most?

CHEEVER: Emotional and intellectual adventurousness. These are unknown countries into which one always steps in fiction.

STILLMAN: How do you feel about innovations in language? The way a story is being told as opposed to the way a character is being defined or the way a plot is being worked out.

CHEEVER: I don't know what you mean by innovations in language. You mean using made-up words?

STILLMAN: I mean speaking in particularly poetic or unpoetic ways, or mixing levels of vocabulary, or tying sentences together in unusual ways, or dipping in and out of standard English and moving into, say, the language of dreams or the language of symbols.

CHEEVER: I'm old enough to recall the death of the word being announced immediately at the end of the First World War, by Gide, subsequently by Huxley, by the editors of *Transition*—the word was no longer competent to deal with our passions, our exaltations and our dismay, we must find something else. So then we had Gertrude Stein, whose contribution was enormous. Then we had automatic writing, and forty years later we again have automatic writing, which is: you write "Bang Bang Yellow Bosh Pow Yellow Yellow Fall." You can take, as far as I can see, perhaps two or three pages of this, and then you realize that you are dealing with a dead language. In short, language has lost its urgency, has lost its ability to enable you to give or to request something from another person. And the instant this is gone, you have a dead language. Dead languages have limited charms, but limited they are. Does that answer your question? Can you think of anyone, for example, who has been a successful experimenter? Stein, I think, is probably the leading light.

STILLMAN: I see that perhaps some of the things that are revered by readers these days you might see as the source of error. I'm thinking for the moment of Joyce and all his experimentation, particularly in *Finnegans Wake*.

CHEEVER: *Finnegans Wake* I find extremely difficult. That seems to be a universal situation. The greatness of *Ulysses*, of course is indisputable. And *Ulysses*, with the exception of some of the Nighttown section, is quite traditional. But my feeling is that the introspective cadence that I have is something I share with almost everyone. One can alter the introspective cadence in prose, as Joyce does in *Ulysses*—and as James did very successfully in all of his fiction. When one reads James, one has to sacrifice the cadence of one's own introspection. And if one's successful at doing this, one is enchanted with James. And when you put down James and come back to your own introspective cadence, it is with this great sense of refreshment. Joyce does this. He does it in the *Dubliners*, he does it in *The Portrait of the Artist as a Young Man*, and he does it extravagantly and triumphantly in *Ulysses*. But one is giving up one's particular habitual cadence for another man's cadence. And this does not seem to me as innovative as it is thought by some people to have been, since one has it in James—in Sterne—and it has appeared in literature before. But *Ulysses* is quite a traditional book.

GIOIA: What do you think of an experiment like Nabokov's *Pale Fire*?

CHEEVER: I think *Pale Fire* is marvelous. "Experimental"? I don't think is quite the word. It's a triumph in inventiveness to write a novel in terms of a footnote to a poem. It's like getting out of a human dilemma. You find yourself in an emotional, or geographical, or even a military situation in which your chances of survival are very limited, and you get out by something as resourceful and inventive as writing a footnote to a poem.

GIOIA: Do you think it's a bad idea for a writer to live in a university?

CHEEVER: I don't know enough about university life, really, to answer that question with any information at all. I found in my own teaching that I become so excited and so absorbed in the work I am getting from the students that it draws off an excess energy. In the two teaching stints (Iowa and Boston) I've not been able to do as much work as I'd like, in many cases no work at all. Because all my excitement is placed in the class. I have no idea what any other teacher feels.

Teaching, after all, is a profession, and an exalted profession, and one can't assume that it is simply a way of making money to continue some other occupation. If one tries to, the students will disabuse you of that idea very quickly.

DILLON: Can you say something about whether or not you do a lot of reading still in some of the older works, whether you find that's still fruitful and helpful for you?

CHEEVER: I don't read as much in the eighteenth century as I would like. It seems to me that I took Fielding intravenously, all of Fielding, including the attacks on Walpole and so forth. My children were told that there was no dirtier word in the language than Walpole. I love Fielding. I love *Tristram Shandy*. I'm not inclined to believe that modern life is incomprehensibly difficult until I pick up a page of Fielding, and it has luminousness and a purity that is lost to us.

STILLMAN: Some people would say that fiction has a social impact, that it not only mirrors its society but also tends to transform it. I wonder if you share that view and, if you do, in what ways you would like to see fiction exert its power over our present society?

CHEEVER: Well, it seems to me that the impact is questionably social. The political burden that literature can carry is inestimably delicate. We have very little good political fiction. I can't, for example, think of a good political novel—that is, a novel that has corrective social power. The spiritual impact is, of course, what one seeks in fiction. It is for the depth of the emotion—to make memory more coherent, more creatively accessible.

DILLON: When you write, are there certain political or social movements that impinge on you sufficiently to actually sense it as you're writing? I take, as an example, the women's movement. Do you think that, in any way, that kind of contemporary movement puts certain pressures on your writing?

CHEEVER: No, I think not at all. I'm old enough to remember the force of the Communist Party in the United States as a literary lever. I was, I suppose, very young, maybe twenty, and named in the *New Masses* as the last voice of the decadent bourgeoisie. Didn't bother me at all. Because I was not concerned with social reconstruction. I was concerned with literature as an intimate and acute means of communication. And the Communist Party was very powerful, or attempted to be very powerful, in literature, as we had a great many novels that presumably were going to change our way of thinking about capitalism. The leading one was something called *Marching, Marching*, by a woman named Clara Weatherwax. It won all the Communist Party prizes, and so forth. It did not change anything at all, excepting perhaps it made Clara Weatherwax more unhappy. It's very difficult to trace—except Machiavelli's *The Prince*—any piece of literature that has had marked social impact.

Marked spiritual impact is something all together different.

STILLMAN: How do you feel about Solzhenitsyn?

CHEEVER: As perhaps you know, I'm a Russian buff, and when I was first in Russia, I think ten years ago, Khrushchev was still first secretary. (I was in Russia when Khrushchev was deposed.) Khrushchev, of course, locked Solzhenitsyn up for *One Day in the Life of Ivan Denisovich*, which I think a beautiful book. I didn't meet him—he was then in the provinces and thought to have cancer. The *First Circle* I also thought a splendid book. The CIA then obviously picked Solzhenitsyn as a man who could be exploited to expose the stupidity, or the cantankerousness, of the Russian government—and without taking into consideration his characteristics as an orthodox Christian. It was unfortunate, I think, that they should have taken a literary character and transformed him into a political one. And that was done. The thing came to a head with the Nobel Prize. They behaved with incredible stupidity, and so I think did we. With the exception of *One Day in the Life of Ivan Denisovich* and *The First Circle*, Solzhenitsyn is virtually unreadable. That he should have been sold as a political identity to the book-buying public in the United States seems to me inexcusable. I've talked with the Russians about it—and, if you know Russians at all, there is a point where you realize that what you thought was a Westernized personality is a complete mystery. But one of the most moving things that was said to me was by a good friend in Moscow, when I was saying, "You are treating Solzhenitsyn as though literature were a province," and she yelled at me, "You don't understand that in my country a great novel is much more important than a great treaty"—which seemed to me the best expression of their attitude. However, Solzhenitsyn is among us, has the strength of character, of faith—and [is], in his own giftedness, evidently to live a very happy life independently both of Brezhnev and the CIA. So it's a happy ending. And what does one look forward to? A new and splendid book from Solzhenitsyn.

STILLMAN: I'm not sure I fully understand. I've been reading *The Gulag Archipelago*.

CHEEVER: Did you like it?

STILLMAN: Of course, it's not fiction, so it's in a totally different domain.

CHEEVER: But it is history written by a novelist. I've not read it, I'm sorry to say. John Updike and I were in Russia together, both of us for the first time, and we were enchanted with the people and the experience. We were there for six weeks. (We were only together, I think, for ten days.) And we were aware of Solzhenitsyn then, of course, and as soon as he was turned into a political pawn, we refrained from signing any papers objecting to the treatment of Solzhenitsyn. John would call me or write, and say, "Well, let's hold off, let's see what's going to happen." Finally, the stupidity and clumsiness and brutality of the Russians was so great that we consulted and agreed to sign a letter, with Dick Wilbur, to the Commissioner of Culture. It was a very gentle letter saying how much we loved the people and the country of Russia, and so forth. And that was absolutely the end (of our reputations there). We were wiped out. I'd received, for ten years, at least twenty-five cards in the neighborhood of the twenty-fifth of December from the Russians, and this year I did not receive a card for the first time in ten years.

STILLMAN: I wonder if there are various subjects or concerns that you have that we have not been able to touch on because we haven't asked the right questions?

CHEEVER: I do feel (an ax I've already ground) that the post-Freudian generation greatly underestimated the creative force of the imagination. And literature—and this is a chestnut I've used before, but I think it works—that literature is our only continuous history of man's struggle to be illustrious and remains our most intimate and acute means of communication.

INDEX OF NAMES

Dana Gioia was born in Los Angeles in 1950. He received his BA and MBA degrees from Stanford University. He also has an MA in Comparative Literature from Harvard University. For fifteen years he worked as a business executive in New York before quitting in 1992 to write full-time. He has published five collections of poetry—*Daily Horoscope* (1986), *The Gods of Winter* (1991), *Interrogations at Noon* (2001) which won the American Book Award, *Pity the Beautiful* (2012), and *99 Poems: New and Selected* (2016) which won the Poets' Prize. Gioia's first critical collection, *Can Poetry Matter?* (1992), was a finalist for the National Book Critics Circle Award. He has also published fifteen anthologies of poetry and fiction. He is the former Poet Laureate of California. Gioia has received the Laetare Medal from Notre Dame University and the Aiken Taylor Award for lifetime contribution to American poetry. From 2003 to 2009 he served as Chairman of the National Endowment for the Arts. Gioia held the Judge Widney Chair of Poetry and Public Culture at the University of Southern California. He divides his time between Los Angeles and Sonoma County, California.